Inclusion:
450 Strategies for Success

A Practical Guide for All Educators Who Teach Students With Disabilities

Peggy A. Hammeken

CORWIN PRESS
A SAGE Publications Company
Thousand Oaks, CA 91320

For information:

Corwin Press
A SAGE Company
2455 Teller Road
Thousand Oaks, California 91320
www.corwinpress.com

SAGE Ltd.
1 Oliver's Yard
55 City Road
London EC1Y 1SP
United Kingdom

SAGE India Pvt. Ltd.
B 1/I 1 Mohan Cooperative
   Industrial Area
Mathura Road, New Delhi 110 044
India

SAGE Asia-Pacific Pte Ltd
33 Pekin Street #02-01
Far East Square
Singapore 048763

Printed in the United States of America.

ISBN: 1-890455-25-3

This book is printed on acid-free paper.

11   12   13   14   15   11   10   9   8   7   6   5   4   3

Table of Contents

Acknowledgements

This book is a collaborative effort on the part of many educators, students, parents and administrators. The ideas have been compiled from actual experiences in inclusive education settings.

I would like to acknowledge the Eden Prairie School District (Eden Prairie, MN) for providing support and encouragement to all staff involved in inclusive education settings. Their contributions and ideas were the foundation for this book. For the revised, updated edition, I want to thank all of the dedicated educators, consultants, service providers, and parents nationwide who have shared their ideas, comments and suggestions.

I would like to also acknowledge my family. Vanessa and Melissa provided encouragement and contributed ideas throughout all stages of the book. This book would not have been possible without my husband, Roberto. His enthusiasm and support is always apparent, even during the difficult stages of the book.

This book is dedicated to my mother, Marlene (1934-1992), who taught me at an early age that all people are equal, regardless of their ethnic background, religion or disability.

ADMINISTRATORS AT SNAILVILLE SCHOOL LAMENT THE SPEED OF CHANGE.

Source: "Ants in His Pants: Absurdities and Realities of Special Education" by Michael F. Giangreco © 1998 Reprinted with permission.

This page may not be reproduced.

"When the world seems large and complex, we need to remember that great world ideals all begin in some home neighborhood."

Konrad Adenauer

A Word from the Author

The passage of the Education for All Handicapped Children Act of 1975 (P.L. 94-142) mandated a free appropriate public education for all children with disabilities. This law also guaranteed due process rights, mandated IEPs and became the core of funding for special education. With P.L. 94-142, the educational system faced the challenge to include all students with disabilities into the general education setting. The law also declared that all students were to be educated in the least restrictive environment. In spite of the law, two educational systems emerged. One educational system was called "regular" and the second "special". As students returned to their home schools, the resource room, often located apart from the general education classroom, became the most widely used placement alternative. In reality, the majority of programs were still separate, but were now located within the same building. During this time period, many students were mainstreamed into the general education setting for classes such as home economics, physical education, the arts, during lunch and recess, or when specific educational criterion was mastered. Since 1975, the educational system has made enormous strides in providing appropriate education for people with disabilities, but nevertheless, there is still a great deal that needs to be accomplished.

The Education for All Handicapped Children Act (EHA) has been revised and updated many times since 1975. EHA was first amended in 1990 by P.L.101-476, which among other things changed the name of the legislation to Individuals with Disabilities Act, commonly referred to as IDEA. The newest amendments to this law are called the Individuals with Disabilities Education Act Amendments of 1997 (P.L. 105-17). These final regulations currently guide school systems in how they design and implement the special education and related service programs. This latest reauthorization includes many modifications to the law. Some of these changes in the latest amendment are significant, while others fine tune the processes already laid out for schools to follow when planning and providing special education services to students with disabilities. Some of the most significant changes in this amendment for the special education process include: participation of students in state and district wide assessment programs; the way in which evaluations are conducted; parent participation in eligibility and placement decisions; increased emphasis upon participation of students in the general education classroom and curriculum with appropriate aids and services; transition planning; voluntary mediation, as a means of resolving conflicts; and discipline of children with disabilities. The regulations for IDEA spell out the procedures and programming that must be provided to children and youth with disabilities in order for States to receive Federal funds. Because States base their individual programs upon the law and its final regulations, it is helpful for you to read and become familiar with the law itself. These documents are available on the Internet at the Office of Special Education Programs (OSEP). For a general overview go the web site for the National Information Center for Children and Youth with Disabilities (NICHCY). This site is an excellent resource for educators and parents. Both web site addresses are listed in the appendix.

In today's schools, the practice of educating all children with and without disabilities together in heterogeneous classrooms often is referred to as inclusive education or simply inclusion. The terms inclusion, full inclusion, and mainstreaming are frequently interchanged. Inclusive education entitles the student to exercise their basic right, the right to be educated in the least restrictive environment. Special education is no longer a place, but a set of services which enable every student to experience success and participate to the greatest extent possible. The set of services developed for individual students is created with the understanding that there is no single "one size fits all" standard. A full continuum of service options is available, but the general education classroom is usually the first placement option even if the student's individual goals is different from those of their peers. When a student is removed from the classroom environment, the school district must be able to justify the removal of the student.

Nationwide, our society is becoming more diverse. This societal change is reflected in the school districts as well. As students in the general education setting become increasingly diverse, current curriculum and material must be adapted to accommodate all students.

Throughout the United States, school districts differ in their acceptance, commitment and implementation of inclusive practices. School districts must define their philosophies. General and special education teachers must plan together for the participation and social integration of students with disabilities. It is no longer a choice of whether or not to include a student. It is the law!

In 2000, this book was revised and updated. Although material has been added and expanded upon, the numbered ideas continue to correspond with the previous edition. Throughout the book, the terms accommodation, adaptation, and modification are often used interchangeably. This is based on the premise that all are types of changes made to curriculum, instruction, or assessment practices in order for students to be successful learners. Therefore, an accommodation for one student may become an adaptation for another.

This book is based on the author's belief that:

Inclusive education can improve the current educational system. With inclusive education, the adaptations and modifications, directed toward students with disabilities, are beneficial to other students in the general education setting as well. These strategies help to improve and individualize the curriculum for all students. The focus of the educational system is placed on the student instead of the curriculum.

Inclusive education helps students become more accepting and sensitive to one another. When students with special needs are included in the general education setting, all students benefit. Students learn to accept one another as contributing members of society, regardless of their abilities or limitations.

Inclusive education encourages collaboration. Both general and special education teachers possess a wealth of information due to their education and experience. Yet in the past, rarely was time allowed to share this information. With inclusive education, the current educational system is no longer two disconnected systems with separate curriculum and goals. With inclusive education, all members of the educational team work together and share knowledge while striving towards a common goal

Inclusive education is not a passing trend. It's the law! Persons with disabilities have often been undervalued in our society. A great amount of time and energy is spent testing, sorting and labeling, oftentimes so we can justify serving, separating, and excluding. There is a great deal to learn from one another. By combining knowledge and expertise, creating partnerships between families and school personnel, the result will be an improved educational system for all.

"We can do anything we want if we stick to it long enough."

Helen Keller

"Let us be a proud nation that takes responsibility for all our children."

Judy Heumann

Introduction

Inclusion! Does the word bring about feelings of excitement and adventure, or does it lead to feelings of fear, anxiety, and apprehension? Conceivably, the word "inclusion" may generate a combination of both positive and negative feelings. But, no matter what the feelings are, rest assured all educators have experienced the same range of emotions at one time or another. The strong feelings associated with the concept of inclusive education often are not directly related to the integration of students into the general education setting. Most educators strongly believe that students with disabilities do belong in the classroom and are entitled to an appropriate education with their peers. Many of the strong feelings directed toward inclusive education often are related to the process of transition and how to manage the transition effectively. The dual educational system in existence for so many years must merge. This is a slow process and will not occur automatically. It will take time, an abundance of energy, a willingness to change, and most of all, an internal belief that inclusive education is truly the best for all students.

This book is developed to focus on inclusive practices for students with disabilities in the general education setting. With the implementation of inclusive education programs in schools nationwide and the development of curriculum adaptations, all students benefit. In today's classroom, these accommodations also benefit students who receive service under Title One, Section 504, and those students who have no "label" but simply need additional support for success.

This book is divided into three sections. The first section contains ideas to help develop and implement an inclusive education program. The implementation phase is crucial to the success of an inclusive education, yet often this area is overlooked. If an existing program is in place, this section includes an abundance of ideas to help improve and/or expand the setting.

The second section of the book includes hundreds of ideas and strategies for modifying and adapting the curriculum. These ideas will help all students in the general education environment. Many of the ideas listed are applicable for all curriculum areas. The words modification and adaptation are used interchangeably, as a modification for one student may be an adaptation for another.

The ideas are numbered for your convenience. When planning, write the number of the idea you would like to implement. This number allows you to quickly reference and document the results. It will save a great amount of time and effort when planning for individual students. Once a change is implemented, maintain a log and document the result. After several weeks, add an additional strategy. If one idea doesn't seem to help the individual student, try another. Remember, since all students are unique, what proves successful for one student will not necessarily be effective for another. Implement only one or two strategies at a time and be sure the student has ample time to adjust, before deciding whether or not the strategy is appropriate. If too many changes are implemented at one time, it will be difficult to document which strategy or combination of strategies is most beneficial. Some students readily adapt to the change while others need additional time.

Whenever the curriculum is adapted or modified, create files and save the materials for future use. Determine a central location where copies of the materials can be cataloged and stored. At the building level, this central location becomes a resource area for both general and special education materials. Some districts have a central resource area. This allows teachers and support staff to easily share materials throughout the district. Also look for resources already available. Contact the publishers of adopted textbooks to see if appropriate supplemental resources are available. Network with colleagues in other schools to see if they have copies of materials on audiocassette before creating your own. When creating materials, check within the community to see if there are adult volunteers who can help.

The final section includes an Appendix with reproducible worksheets and resources to assist with inclusive education. Use the worksheets as they appear in the book, or adapt them to meet the individual needs of the program. Also included is a list of national organizations. These organizations often specialize in specific areas and will be able to answer questions or help with referrals to the appropriate agencies. Oftentimes, they have inexpensive (sometimes free) resources available.

Good luck with your inclusive program! You will make a difference in the lives of many.

"The past cannot be changed. The future is yet in your power."

Mary Pickford

EXCLUSION + EXCUSES = "EXCLUSES"
COMMON REASONS FOR AVOIDING INCLUSIVE EDUCATION.

Source: "Ants in His Pants: Absurdities and Realities of Special Education"
by Michael F. Giangreco © 1998 Reprinted with permission.

This page may not be reproduced

"If you think you're too small to make a difference, you obviously have never been in bed with a mosquito!"

Michele Walker

Chapter One

Getting Started

Do you want to implement an inclusive education program, but have no idea of how to begin? Have you ever wanted to include a student into the general education setting but have been unable due to difficulties with scheduling? Have you encountered times when a student should be included in the classroom, but extra support was unavailable? These are common concerns frequently expressed by educators. Inclusive education settings do not just occur. Proper implementation of a program takes time, preparation, and extensive planning. Whether you are in the preliminary stages of planning, or have a successful program in place, you will find information in this chapter to help with all stages of the program development.

Ideally, inclusive education programs are developed during the spring for the upcoming school year. When planned in the spring, students can be grouped, teachers selected, and when the new school year begins, all systems are in place and ready! This is the ideal situation, but not always the reality. Often teachers arrive in the fall and are asked to implement a program. Since student placements were previously determined, this situation is more difficult, but not impossible. When beginning in the fall, start on a small scale. Implement some of the strategies with a few students, or focus on the grade or subject area with the largest concentration of students. If a program is already in place, both general and special education teachers will find many ideas to improve and expand the existing program.

This chapter outlines a basic plan for the implementation of a successful inclusive education setting. If an inclusive education program is not in place, work through ideas 1-27 as a special education team (with administrative support) before presenting the concept to the entire school. It is crucial for the special education department to have a strong and realistic overview of the students, their needs, and the support available. With this in mind, the program needs to be designed not only to meet the needs of the students, but also within the context of the number of educators and paraprofessionals available. This becomes the foundation for the program. In an ideal world, schools would have unlimited budgets, staff, and support services available. But, in the real world, the foundation needs to be laid with the available resources. Therefore, the initial groundwork needs to be developed by the special education department and administration. Usually, at this stage the general education teachers are not involved in the process. The reason for this is simple. General education teachers have an understanding of the amount of direct/indirect service and support provided to their individual classrooms, but usually do not have a picture of the overall program. Nor would we expect them to. Therefore, the information needs to be gathered, analyzed and compiled by the special education department. Once the foundation is laid, the plan is then presented to the remainder of the staff. At this time, there will be changes to the plan, but these changes will be made within the foundation established. The Appendix includes several worksheets to assist with the organization of the program.

Developing a Plan

Each school system is unique. Perhaps you teach in a large school with many special education teachers, specialists and support staff, or possibly a small school where you are the only special education teacher in the department. Whether the school is large or small, a plan is needed. In heavily populated schools with large special education departments, oftentimes, several special education teachers choose to transition toward inclusive education, while the others remain in a self contained environment, providing the service to students who will transition at a later time. Some schools opt to transition all students at once. Still others prefer to begin at the earliest grade level and add a grade level each year. Inclusive education is a process that requires the structure of the educational system to change.

Whether inclusive education is implemented on a small scale, or with the entire special education population, the time to begin is now! The first step in the process is to develop a plan. The special education department usually initiates the plan. Although inclusive education encompasses the entire staff, the special education department must first determine the overall needs of the program. The groundwork needs to be laid. Here are a few questions to think about and discuss. What is the vision? How many students are currently served in special education? Do we want to start the program with a small or large number of students? How many paraprofessionals are available to help support the students? How can the students be placed into classrooms with adequate support? How should the students be grouped? How will a continuum of services be provided and who will provide service to students outside of the inclusive classroom? What are some of the barriers we will encounter? These are not easy questions to answer.

First, the plan must meet the needs of the students, staff, and parents, and incorporate the philosophy of the school district. Every program will look different due to the unique needs of the individual student and the daily classroom schedules. It would be wonderful if a simple blueprint existed for the development of inclusive schools, but that will never be the case. Often school districts spend large amounts of money for consultants to assist in the development of individual programs. There are advantages to using consultants. First, the consultant can provide examples of various models developed in similar settings. Issues can be addressed objectively, as the consultant is not directly involved with the individual school system. But, in the end, the most successful programs are developed by the staff after visiting area schools, working with consultants and compiling all of the data. The "experts" are those people who work in the school environment and are involved with the students on a day-to-day basis. The reason for the success of these programs is simple. The educators, support staff, and parents understand the needs and the unique dynamics of the building, which strongly influence the program development. Whether you are an individual or part of a committee, you are now an "expert". No one knows the school climate, students, or the dynamics of the staff better than the staff working within the building.

To begin, schools approach inclusive education in many ways. In some districts, several teachers who are ready for the transition may develop and pilot a program for one grade level or subject area. In other districts, committees may develop a school wide plan. Whether you are an individual or a committee of individuals, the following guidelines will help tailor a program to meet the needs of your environment. Worksheet 1 in the Appendix provides and overview of the following section.

1. Develop a vision. Think about the following questions: What would the ideal program look like? Where in the process would you like to be in one month? Three months? Six months? What are the long term goals? Keep in mind that while including students in the classroom, some students need a continuum of services. With inclusive education, the first option is the least restrictive environment (usually the classroom), and only when the services provided in this setting (consultation, adaptations, the use of a paraprofessional) are ineffective, is the student moved to a more restrictive placement.

2. List the benefits and possible barriers to inclusive education within the building. Worksheet 2 lists some possible benefits and barriers. Use this worksheet and add additional items or create your own on Worksheet 3 and compare the responses.

   Note: Later when the information is presented to the entire staff, use Worksheet 3 in the Appendix. The staff response frequently parallels the response of the Special Education Department. When this activity is completed with the building staff, you will have some suggestions of ways to overcome some of these barriers and obstacles. Worksheet 3, located in the Appendix, can be used as an individual worksheet or as a transparency to compile the group response.

3. Visit schools in the area that have inclusive education programs. Observe the programs in action. Talk with teachers, service providers, and the paraprofessionals involved. Take notes! Learn from their experiences. Remember, often a negative experience can be made positive with a few changes. Call the Department of Education in your state to find out which school districts are involved in pilot programs or have received grants to implement programs. Set appointments to visit these schools. Also inquire at local universities about current programs. Frequently, universities receive grant money to

develop training programs. These programs are often available to school districts for a minimal fee.

4. Read current research, journal articles, or books related to inclusive education. Search the Internet for information. Some key words for the search include: Special Education, ERIC, Inclusive Education, or you may search for a specific disability. When searching a specific disability, frequently you will access the national organization related to the disability. These organizations have vast amounts of information and often have links to additional related Web sites. If you find an exceptionally good site, add a bookmark, or you may never find it again! Additional information can be accessed through the United States Department of Education or the Department of Education in your state. The Appendix includes additional books, resources, and a list of organizations to help you.

5. Once steps 1-4 are complete, it is time to develop the building plan. You have a vision and have discovered there will be barriers and obstacles to either overcome or work around. You know what is occurring in neighboring schools and districts. A collection of resources has been compiled. For future reference, compile this information into a three-ring binder.

Grouping of Students

Due to the increasing number of students in special education and the limited resources, both human and monetary, the most feasible option is to group students. Obviously, students need to be grouped carefully. In order to do this, target a specific grade or subject area. If, at this time, you are the only teacher moving toward inclusive education, target a grade level or subject area with a large number of students. It is easier to work with a large number of students at one grade level than small groups of students at multiple grade levels. If the entire special education team is moving toward providing service in the classroom, determine how to divide the caseloads. If dividing by grade level, the caseloads will not be even. Keep in mind that it is easier to work with 18 students at one grade level (only one curriculum to master) than two grade levels with five students. Each teacher should work with the fewest number of grade levels or subject areas as possible. When working in several grade levels or multiple classrooms, the schedules must be staggered allowing for support across the building.

Often inclusive education programs are difficult to manage because students are placed individually into classrooms. With only one student per classroom, there is insufficient time to consult with teachers, provide adequate accommodations, or provide the amount of service predetermined by the IEP. Grouping students is not for the convenience of educators, which some critics believe. Students must be grouped, as school districts do not have sufficient funds to hire an adequate amount of staff to support one student per classroom. When considering placement, do not group students by handicapping conditions. You do not want to develop a resource room within the general education classroom. Consider the use of cross-categorical groups. Several examples of cross-categorical groups follow:

* A high need student, (with documented paraprofessional time in the IEP) possibly could be placed with students who need only curriculum adaptations and minimal support. The paraprofessional is able to assist the high need student and provide support to the other students at the same time.

* Students who receive service for math only could possibly be grouped.

* A student with a behavior disorder could be placed with a student who needs minimal support, or with a student who functions several years below grade level and if appropriate become a peer tutor.

* A student with a mild/moderate cognitive delay (who requires an alternative curriculum) may be placed with a group of students who require only curriculum modifications for reading and written language.

The groupings depend upon the individual needs of each student, which are determined by the IEP. Periodically, a situation occurs where the student must have an individual classroom placement. However, for the majority of students, cross-categorical groupings work well.

The implementation phase is one of the most important areas to consider when developing inclusive education programs. Unfortunately, it is also the greatest challenge. In a perfect world, school districts would have sufficient staff members to serve all students without grouping. Rarely does this occur. When students are grouped, the special education staff is able to spend more time in the classroom, which results in more appropriate accommodations and enhanced support for the individual student. As the students move into the second year of the program, some will need more support, others less, and the groups can be adjusted accordingly.

It is important to have an administrator present when grouping students. The administrator has an overview of all students and often knows confidential information or of special circumstances that prohibits specific student placements.

Before you begin to group the students, write each name on a Post-It Note™. The names can be rearranged easily on a blackboard. Experiment with various student groups before finalizing the placement. Keep in mind that neither the special nor general education population will ever fit into perfect groups, therefore, look for manageable groups. Place yourself in the position of the classroom teacher. If a combination of students is difficult to manage in a special education setting, it will also be difficult in a classroom setting. The following suggestions offer some guidelines to grouping. Experiment with various combinations. Once again, do not group the students by disability.

6. Review the IEP for each student. Look for the student's strengths. When reviewing files, write the area(s) of service, minutes and the amount of paraprofessional time documented in the IEP. You will need this information when you develop the plan. Use Worksheets 4 and 5 in the Appendix.

7. Group the students at each grade level into the smallest number of classrooms possible. A recommendation is 2-5 students per classroom, depending upon the needs. With grouping, communication increases, as will the amount of direct service. Fifteen minutes in a classroom with one student is not as beneficial as one hour with four students.

The larger time block allows more flexibility for both general and special education teachers.

8. There are several options to consider when grouping students. Consider the following:

   * Academic needs
   * Reading levels
   * Learning styles
   * Math placement
   * Problem solving skills
   * Work habits
   * Organizational skills
   * Behavioral goals and objectives
   * Content or subject area

9. When grouping by reading levels, keep in mind that students who need minimal adaptations may be able to work with a paraprofessional, if no teaching is required. Use Worksheets 6 and 7 to help with student groups.

10. When appropriate, group students who receive adaptive physical education, speech/language service, occupational therapy, physical therapy or other related services. Often these services are provided in a separate location. When students are grouped, coordination of these related services is easier, as the general education teacher often is able to schedule the academics around these support services. If possible, incorporate the related services into the general education setting. For example, incorporate occupational therapy service into the written language block or at the elementary level into a handwriting program. The adaptive physical education teacher may lend support to the regular physical education teacher or perhaps team teach. The speech and language clinician may support the student during language arts by helping the student organize thoughts or lend support to specific vocabulary exercises.

11. Group students who require daily monitoring of organizational skills, or participate in a daily check-in or check-out program. Remember, when working with a small number of teachers, communication increases, which results in a better and more consistent program for each individual student.

12. Students in the due process system should be grouped into a classroom if the preliminary data suggests the student may qualify.

13. Review placement files for new students. If there are questions about the file, call the previous school before assigning the student to a classroom.

Paraprofessional Time

Now that students have tentatively been grouped into classrooms, it is time to determine the amount of paraprofessional minutes for each group of students. A comment heard frequently is, "We simply do not have enough paraprofessionals to provide adequate support for the students." When students are not grouped, paraprofessionals are assigned to various classrooms for relatively short periods of time. In many cases, when the paraprofessional arrives, the general education teacher is giving instruction or completing a lecture. If additional time is not built into the paraprofessional's schedule, the end result is often loss of support to the student. Flexibility is very important.

When students are grouped and paraprofessionals are placed strategically within these groups, more direct service is available, resulting in increased support for the student. The program must be created with the allotment of paraprofessional time previously determined in the IEP. Also, there must be time for the special education teachers to collaborate with both paraprofessionals and general education teachers daily. The less people involved in each segment of the program, the more efficient the program becomes. Communication is the key to successful inclusion.

Paraprofessionals are vital to inclusive education. In many districts the number of paraprofessionals exceeds the number of special education teachers. These hardworking adults provide service to many of the most complex and challenging students in the school, yet often they are unsupervised and receive limited training. The role of the paraprofessional is to provide service and support to individual students or groups of students. This may include reteaching a previously learned skill, providing academic, social and emotional support, and helping students with personal care. The role of the paraprofessional is not that of a surrogate teacher. When determining the amount of service for paraprofessionals, keep the following in mind:

14. Consider the allotted paraprofessional minutes very carefully. Strategically place paraprofessionals assigned to specific high need students into classrooms where other students will also benefit.

15. Students who need daily accommodations for assignments, curriculum support, or reteaching may be grouped with a paraprofessional. The paraprofessional cannot provide direct initial instruction, but can reteach and reinforce the skills previously taught, make curriculum adaptations (under the direction of the general or special education teacher), and provide support with daily assignments.

16. If there are blocks of open time in the paraprofessional's schedule, mark it as "flexible time". Once the program is implemented, general education teachers may use this time for additional support for the students with special needs. In this manner, support is extended to other curriculum areas. Some schools have established a time block and specific classroom as a "support room". Staffing of this room often is voluntary. Some schools rotate the duties between special and general education teachers, and paraprofessionals. Others schools have staffed this area with parent volunteers. Any student who needs additional support or testing may use the room. This helps all students, not only those with special needs.

17. Flexible scheduling works in some districts. The paraprofessional is employed for a specific number of hours per week. The hours are used as needed and may

change on a daily basis. This increases the flexibility of the program. It works well for paraprofessionals who are employed two to three hours per day. Some schools allow the paraprofessional to "comp" time if needed for special projects or field trips. Some of the more fortunate districts have money set aside to increase hours as needed. Check with the district to see if there are any options for scheduling.

18. Schedule a minimum of 10 minutes per day for the general education teacher and paraprofessional to meet and plan. The paraprofessional is a vital member of the team. In the Resource section of this book, there are several books listed specifically for the paraprofessional. *Inclusion: An Essential Guide for the Paraprofessional* is the paraprofessional component to this series.

19. Develop a tentative schedule for the paraprofessional(s). The schedule should include the total number of hours required for the program. These minutes are directly correlated to the Individualized Education Plan. If there are additional hours available, determine as a group where additional service is needed. Remember to include consultation time in the schedule. Worksheet 8 in the Appendix will help with the calculation of the paraprofessional hours.

Scheduling

Now it is time to look at the daily structure of the program. Gather copies of the schedules for the grade level or subject areas selected. Read the following ideas about scheduling several times before beginning. As a group, discuss the types of scheduling which may work for the individual environment. Look at sample Worksheet 9 in the Appendix for ideas. Worksheet 10 is a blank worksheet. It provides a basic outline from which to work.

Remember this is a preliminary schedule. Once general education teachers volunteer to be part of the program, there will be additional changes, but often these changes are worked out between the individual teachers involved.

20. The majority of students receive service for the reading and written language blocks. It is important to stagger the time blocks on the schedule so special education teachers are available to provide direct service to the inclusive classrooms. Here are some examples:

   * If two classes have the same reading and language arts block, consider grouping students who work with the paraprofessional into one of the blocks and schedule the special education teacher into the other. If paraprofessional time is not available, the two (or more) classroom teachers and the special education teacher will need to find a time which is favorable for both schedules.

   * At the secondary level, reading and written language affects most of the academic areas. Stagger the time blocks. Once the general education teachers volunteer or are selected to work in the inclusive setting, many choose to collaboratively plan lessons and work as a team. Teaming takes on many forms. Often, one team member plans a lesson collaboratively with the special education teacher, while the other may plan a large group activity, work on individual projects or show a video or film. The direct instruction and group activities are then rotated allowing for more support. When determined in advance, schedules can be planned accordingly, which in turn, increases the flexibility of the program and the amount of time for direct service. The special education teacher and paraprofessional can rotate between classes as needed.

21. It is very important that the special education teacher or paraprofessional is present during the initial instruction. Often, staff members feel this is wasted time, therefore,

they do not schedule in these additional minutes. But, this time is beneficial for several reasons:

* It allows the general education teacher maximum flexibility to monitor and adjust assignments. When lesson changes occur, they do not have to be explained to the special education person at a later time.

* The special education person is also able to determine the style of instruction and formulate ways to reteach or clarify the instruction if needed.

* It is an optimum to observe students in a group setting.

22. Determine the number of students who receive service for math. If the students are grouped for math instruction, it may be possible to place the students with math goals into one classroom and team teach the subject. If the students are not grouped for math, there are several options: divide the special education time between two classrooms; group the students with math IEPs into the same homeroom; use paraprofessional time to assist with the coverage of the various groups. At the secondary level, often students with IEPs take a fundamental math course. If this is an option, this course could be team taught.

23. Determine the students' needs for the entire school day. Previously, students have been served mainly in the isolated areas of reading, written language, math and speech/language. These four areas impact the entire school day. Incorporate service into the appropriate academic blocks.

24. Create a flexible time slot in the schedule. It does not need to be a large block of time. The general education teachers may use this time block to incorporate special projects, lessons, or alternate testing procedures as needed. This time block may also be used as a preparation, observation,

or testing block. Oftentimes, special education teachers do not schedule lunch breaks, as they need to accommodate many different schedules. A lunch break is needed during the day. If this is the case, speak with the general education teachers and decide how schedules can be altered or rotated to provide a specific break in the schedule. Grade levels have specific lunch blocks and special education professionals need to do the same.

25. Schedule time each day, before or after school, to meet with each general education teacher. This may be an informal arrangement. Changes in daily lesson plans can be made during this time. You will be amazed at the number of items that can be discussed during a five-minute time block. Since many special education meetings occur before school, be sure there is a definite ending time scheduled and honor this time. A lack of communication will cause the program to deteriorate rapidly.

   With inclusive education, educators are expected to collaborate in ways which have not previously been encountered. Not only finding the time to talk is important, but the way in which ideas and requests are communicated is very important. Most educators have not been trained to supervise other adults, yet in this new system, educators are often responsible to not only supervise, but to evaluate the paraprofessionals. This may be an area where staff development is needed.

26. Staff involvement is important! Look for additional ways to incorporate the special education department into the classroom environment. Some simple ideas may include reading aloud to the class several times per week, participating in special projects, class rewards or field trips. As involvement increases, students see special education as an integral part of the classroom.

27. Try to schedule daily preparation time. This time is easier to schedule at the middle and secondary level as classes meet during specific time blocks. At the elementary level,

it is more difficult as the school day does not have these natural divisions. If you are unable to schedule a preparation/testing block, ask general education teachers to advise you, in advance, when there are open breaks in the schedule. Often unplanned events occur and special education service is not needed. When notified in advance, this time may be allocated as a preparation or testing block. Additional preparation and testing time often occur during group activities, movies, speakers, field trips, art activities or special programs.

Presenting the Inclusion Plan

Congratulations! The plan is ready to present. The plan includes:

* Vision and goals of the program
* Benefits and possible barriers
* Target group of students (small or large)
* Number of staff and paraprofessionals needed to put the plan into effect
* Classroom schedules for the grade levels or subject areas selected.

This is the basic plan. Read it carefully. Add any additional, relevant information. Now, the time has arrived to present the plan to the principal or supervisor. Submit the outline in a written format. Include all the preliminary compiled data: benefits/barriers, paraprofessional time, possible groups and schedules. Worksheet 11, located in the Appendix, outlines the information that could be included in the presentation. With this vast amount of information, the special education staff is prepared to answer many of the questions that may arise.

Once the administration has approved the plan, it is time to present an overview of inclusive education and the preliminary plan to the staff. First determine who will present the plan: the special services department, the administrators, or a combination of the two. Often schools invite the special services director or coordinator to this initial meeting to answer specific questions relating to the law.

As a special education team, hours have been spent in preparation for this meeting, but for the general education staff this is the first information session. Although some general questions will be asked during the initial session, the majority of teachers need to process the information and reflect on how it will personally impact their individual situation before questions will be generated. Therefore, a follow-up session should be scheduled to answer specific questions.

The staff is now aware that students with disabilities, special education teachers, paraprofessionals and consultants will be active participating members in the general education setting. The entire school will be affected to some degree, but the greatest challenge is for the general and special education teachers directly involved in the program.

Now the big question! Is participation voluntary or are the general education teachers selected by the administration? Although it is done both ways, attitude plays an important role in the success of the program. A positive attitude is crucial to the success of any new program. Oftentimes, the negative attitudes encountered are not directly related to providing service to those with special needs, but are related to how an individual responds to and accepts change. There are a small percentage of people who thrive and embrace the chance to implement a new program. These people enjoy the challenge and excitement of trying something new and different. Others may have a "wait and see" attitude. These individuals prefer to observe first and make sure that the program is effective and is in the best interest of the students before investing their time and energy. These individuals prefer to come on board once they have seen the movement of the program. Still there are others who do not want to implement a change, due to upcoming retirement, career change, or personal reasons that have not been shared.

The following is based on the premise that the entire target group of teachers is part of the planning session until step #34 when participants are asked to volunteer. For example, if third grade is the target level, all third grade teachers must participate until step #34. Once step #34 is reached, only those who either volunteer or are selected will participate. It is important that the entire grade level is involved because, whether or not they participate directly in the program, there will be some changes that impact the entire grade level. For example, if the entire grade level has reading instruction in the morning, some must be willing to change their schedule to the afternoon so the special education department is able to serve all of the students in the program. Depending upon the target group of teachers selected, you will need to monitor and adjust the following ideas.

28. Meet with the target group of teachers. This meeting should include all service providers for the selected target group of students. List the new questions and ideas. Try to find the answers to the questions and incorporate the ideas into the plan. Since there is no blueprint to follow with inclusive education, a definitive answer may not be available.

29. With guidance from your administrator or supervisor, select 2-3 teachers from the target group to review the revisions and make any further corrections.

30. Be open to all new ideas and suggestions. Others will add valuable insights from perspectives that may not have occurred to you. Incorporate these ideas and suggestions. Make the necessary changes and revise the plan.

31. By this time, the plan has been revised several times. Present the final draft to the target group. Once again, discuss the benefits of an inclusive education program and possible barriers that may be encountered. Share any creative ways learned from others or read about which may help to alleviate some of these obstacles.

32. Now the plan is complete. Present the proposed schedules that have been developed.

33. Teachers must be aware of the increased daily time commitment. Both general and special education teachers need to consult and plan frequently, especially during the initial stages of the program. Once the program has been implemented and teachers involved know one another, the amount of time spent during each planning session may decrease, but the sessions will still occur frequently.

34. Allow time for the general education teachers to discuss the plan. Be prepared to meet again and discuss any concerns or further questions that arise. At the second meeting, ask teachers to think about whether or not they

would like to participate in the program for the upcoming year.

35. Now is the time to ask for volunteers to participate in the program. Once a teacher volunteers, the teacher is committed to the success of the program! Commitment is important!

    If volunteers are not an option, the administration will need to determine the program participants.

36. A belief that every student has the right to be included in the general education classroom, a positive attitude, enthusiasm, a sense of humor, and the willingness to make a change are the key elements of a successful inclusive education setting.

Inservice and Training

Attitude plays an important role in the success of the program. In order for a successful inclusive education program to take place, all educators must be enthusiastic and ready to implement the change. Often the fear associated with any change is the fear of the unknown. Therefore, as with any school wide change, training is an important component.

Inservice and training may be implemented in many ways. The majority of universities now offer courses related to inclusive education. There are many consultants who design training to meet the specific needs of individual buildings. Call the local university or Department of Education in the state to inquire about course offerings and availability. The Resource Section of this book lists materials which can be used for staff development and training. Staff development videos require a substantial initial investment, but the videos can be used again and again for large and small group presentations and for new staff members.

In order to provide appropriate training, the needs of the staff must be determined. Training at the building level should be geared toward the specific needs of the staff and the individual building.

37. Survey the entire staff. Worksheet 12 is a sample survey form. This survey will help to assess the needs and concerns within the building. Design the inservice to meet these needs. Do not forget to survey those individuals who work in the areas of transportation, food service, custodial service, and the hallway and playground monitors. It is beneficial for a member of the special education team to meet individually with each group and answer questions related to the various school settings.

Inservice at the building level may be developed around some of these frequently asked questions.

Overview of Inclusive Education

* What is inclusive education? How does it differ from mainstreaming?

* Why is inclusive education important?

* What are the federal and state guidelines related to inclusive education?

* What is the district philosophy?

* How do we include students in the general education environment and yet meet all of their needs?

Collaboration

* What is an effective team? How can we work together to form effective teams?

* What are the roles and responsibilities of each person in an effective inclusion setting?

❋ What are various teaching models that can be used in a collaborative setting?

❋ How can we creatively find additional time to plan together?

❋ How can we increase the communication in a collaborative setting?

Modifying and Adapting Curriculum

❋ What are accommodations?

❋ How do we modify and adapt the curriculum?

❋ What is the difference between a modification and adaptation?

❋ How can curriculum be adapted when a large discrepancy exists between the general education materials and the students' current levels of performance?

❋ Who is responsible for making the modifications and adapting the curriculum?

Paraprofessionals in the Classroom

❋ What are the roles and responsibilities of the paraprofessional in the classroom?

❋ Who is responsible to guide the paraprofessional?

* Who is responsible for establishing and implementing discipline guidelines for the student in the general education setting when a paraprofessional is present?

* If the student is absent from class, what is the responsibility of the paraprofessional?

* How will the planning time be incorporated into the paraprofessional's day?

* Should the paraprofessional be included in the evaluation of the students? Who is responsible to evaluate the performance of the paraprofessional?

Inservice is an important part of all inclusive education programs. Although inservice is highlighted in this chapter, it should be provided whenever needed. All inservices do not need to be directed towards the entire staff. Many can be presented in small group sessions as the need arise.

Setting Up an Inclusive Classroom

Once the plan has been initiated, the space within the classroom needs to be reorganized to accommodate the extra person (people) in the classroom environment. The classroom set-up depends upon the types of teaching that will take place.

In order for a team to function successfully, the team members should hold the belief that team teaching provides a more effective teaching environment, which in turn benefits all students, not only those with special needs. There are several traits that will help professionals work together collaboratively. These important traits include flexibility, professionalism, the desire to work with others, respect for one another and of course, a sense of humor. Educators in a team situation must be able to listen to one another, communicate effectively, and hold common goals and expectations for students.

There are three main types of teaching that occur in inclusive settings: team teaching, supportive teaching, and supplemental teaching. There are hundreds of variations to these three models and depending upon the resource, it may be referred to by a different name. For our purposes, the terms team, supportive, and supplemental teaching will be used. These terms are simple and self-explanatory. In some classrooms, educators agree to use one main teaching style. In others, educators move between the three styles depending upon the outcome for the student and the type of lesson. The style is determined by the needs of the students and the teachers' comfort level.

Team Teaching: In a team teaching environment, two (or more) staff members work to plan, develop, and teach the lesson. The role and responsibility is determined by those involved. Just as general education teachers often co-teach a lesson, general and special education teachers often do the same.

Supportive Teaching: In a supportive teaching environment, the student receives the basic instruction from the general education teacher. Modifications and instructional support are provided to the student within the classroom setting by the special education teacher. The paraprofessional provides support to the students under the direction of the general or special education teacher.

Supplemental Teaching: In a supplemental teaching environment, the special education teacher or paraprofessional provides reinforcement and reteaching as needed. When assignments cannot be modified or the lesson is not appropriate, a separate curriculum may also be implemented.

The design of the classroom environment depends upon the type of teaching system that will be used, which of course is determined by the needs of the students. The following list provides some ideas that have worked in inclusive settings. Use Worksheet 13 located in the Appendix to provide guidelines for setting up the classroom environment.

38. Determine which teaching environment meets the needs of the selected group of students. Some teachers co-plan and teach the lesson, others prefer to have one teach while the other provides support and yet others prefer to divide the

class into two smaller groups. The teaching strategies vary throughout the day depending upon the structure of the class, the lesson and the individuals (both students and teachers) involved.

39. If you anticipate large amounts of supportive or supplemental teaching to take place, establish a teaching area in the classroom. If table space is not available, a quiet area of the classroom with an ample supply of clipboards will work, although it is not ideal.

40. A table placed outside the classroom is beneficial. Some students prefer to work in small groups outside the classroom because it is less distracting.

41. A study carrel is useful. Portable study carrels, made of corrugated cardboard, can be easily stored when not in use. This benefits the student who is easily distracted.

42. When designing the class seating charts, the students who receive support service should be seated in an area that allows the special education teacher or paraprofessional to access the students without disturbing the rest of the class. No more alphabetical seating!

43. Designate a specific area to leave notes, schedules changes and other pertinent information. Be sure to check it daily.

44. Keep a basket or box of necessary supplies in each classroom. In addition to the basic supply of pencils, pens, markers, and highlighters, include folders to organize copies of lesson plans, personal copies of the Teacher's Guides and additional supplemental materials.

45. Purchase a pushcart and establish a classroom on wheels! It is a great way to keep the supplemental materials close at hand.

46. A file cabinet in the classroom helps keep material and files close at hand. Most teachers will reorganize a space

or provide a drawer in their individual cabinets. If no space is available, the most economical method is to use a file box or inexpensive file folder purchased from a local office supply store.

47. Post a daily schedule in both the general and special education areas. This allows people to find you when necessary.

48. When working in various classrooms, it may be difficult to find you during the day. A pager is a practical solution, especially for teachers of students with severe behavior difficulties. In case of a crisis, the special education teacher can be located immediately. The principal, social worker, or psychologist may be an appropriate backup person in case a situation arises where you are unable to leave. Devise a system.

49. Physically move into the general education area during the school day. A desk may be placed in or near the classrooms at the elementary level. If you are a secondary teacher and work in a specific area such as English, consider placing a desk or worktable in the English Department. For a successful inclusive education program to occur, you need to be close to the students' classrooms during the school day. The more visible you are, the better the communication between the adults.

50. Keep a central file of modified materials and ideas. Store supplemental units and audiocassettes in this file. This will enable the general education teacher to find materials when you are not available. Better yet, make two copies of everything, one for special education and one for general education. If you are really ambitious, send a copy of the materials to the special education administration office. This would help all teachers throughout the district!

51. Develop a centrally located professional library of materials. Include books, videos, reference materials, and

community services on the list. There are many excellent staff development videos available. This is an excellent way for teachers to learn more about a specific subject without having to read an entire text. Videos may also lend support for small group training. Be sure to have a sign-out sheet available. It's amazing how quickly materials disappear.

52. Review all new student records before deciding on placement. Carefully check the files for special education data. If the student received special education service in the past or it looks as though a referral is likely, place the student into the appropriate classroom.

53. As new students are added during the school year, the program becomes more complex and schedules must be coordinated between more people. This is difficult, but not impossible. On the positive side, the majority of new students qualifying for special education often are not placed until January. By this time, the existing program is in operation and running smoothly! Students are more responsible, comfortable with their placements and have become more independent. Of course, if luck is really on your side, the qualifying student will be in a classroom where a program is already in place.

Working as a Team

Educators spend hours each week meeting with parents, colleagues and other adult professionals in the educational system. When the school day begins, teaching takes on real meaning. The classroom becomes an animated stage with one adult performer and an active participating audience of students. When a special education teacher or paraprofessional becomes a part of the group, the dynamics of the entire group may change.

Not all adults are comfortable with another adult in their classroom. Trust will develop. The working dynamics of the program will change as the comfort level increases. In most situations, new friendships and bonds are formed, although, this is not always the case. It is important to remember the ultimate goal of the educational merger is to provide a successful educational experience for the student. As adults, it is important to respect one another as professionals and strive to reach the common goal. With time, an educational team will evolve in place of the two separate educational systems.

54. All teachers have distinct teaching and discipline styles. When working in a specific grade level or subject area, you may observe a strategy which will help others teaching the same unit. Before sharing, ask the teacher for permission. Also, remember that everyone has good and bad days. Focus on the positive.

55. Collaboration is important! Special and general educators frequently view situations differently because of their educational background and experience. This is important in an inclusive setting! As a special educator you are an advocate for the student with special needs. The general educator is an advocate for all of the students in the classroom. If the program is to be successful, educators must collaborate effectively. One of the greatest benefits of inclusive education is the knowledge acquired from working together!

56. Be sure time is scheduled daily to meet with classroom teachers. This time can be used to make changes in lesson plans and schedules. Extreme flexibility is very important! This time should be listed as a priority. In order for inclusive education to work, teachers must talk daily.

57. If possible, work at the same grade level or in the same subject area for at least two years. The first year is a learning experience for everyone. You create a new team, experiment with new teaching strategies, implement training for staff and spend many hours adapting and modifying the curriculum. You learn a tremendous amount from trying new ideas, adapting the old ones and teaching together. The first year in an inclusive setting is comparable to the first year in a new school system.

Everything is new! The second year is much easier for the educational team. You are now an active participating member of the general education team, inservice is minimal, the roles are defined, and the modifications and adaptations can be reused.

58. In a successful inclusive education program, the general education teachers, parents, and students are the strongest advocates.

Follow Up

Once the program is established, it is important to obtain follow up information from the teachers, paraprofessionals, parents, and students. Questionnaires are a simple way to assess. When surveys are used frequently, small problems are discovered before they become problematic. These surveys may also help determine staff development needs. Use Worksheets 14-17 to survey the students, parents, paraprofessionals and teachers in the program.

59. Compile the information received from the surveys. If a parent indicates a concern, call to discuss it. Determine whether the concerns expressed are isolated to a specific classroom (and should be discussed individually) or whether it is a program concern and should be addressed as a team. Analyze the student surveys. Talk to students individually. Look at the needs of the paraprofessionals and decide whether concerns are isolated or whether it affects all of the paraprofessionals. Determine whether or not further inservice is needed.

"Coming together is a beginning, staying together is progress, and working together is success!"

Henry Ford

THE EVOLUTION OF SWIMMING LESSONS:
SURPRISINGLY SIMILAR TO THE EVOLUTION
OF INCLUDING STUDENTS WITH
DISABILITIES IN GENERAL EDUCATION.

Source: "Flying By the Seat of Your Pants; More Absurdities and Realities of Special Education"
by Michael F. Giangreco © 1999 Reprinted with permission.

This page may not be reproduced

"We see a future where young people learn in different ways but all are expected to learn to higher standards."

Judy Huemann

Chapter Two

Accommodations for the Student with Special Needs

In order for a student to be successful in the classroom environment, the curriculum must be adapted to meet the student's needs. The IEP goals focus on the student's limitations, therefore, in order to successfully accommodate the student, the strengths need to be determined. When adapting the curriculum, the following should be addressed:

* What is the goal for this student in this academic area?
* What are the student's strengths?
* Will this accommodation assist the student in reaching the final goal?

Accommodations usually fall within the realm of one of the following four categories:

The activity or content is reinforced. In this category, supplemental support is provided to the student. This additional support enables the student to complete the classroom assignments and to fulfill the class requirements. Previewing, preteaching and reteaching of some assignments may be necessary. Supplemental aids such as study guides, outlines, and audiocassettes of the materials may be provided. Direct instruction is usually provided by the general education teacher and additional support from the special education department.

The activity or the content is modified. In this category, the adaptations are made to the actual material or content of the curriculum. The number of outcomes in a specific content area may be reduced. The student may be provided with additional time to complete assignments. Assignments may be adjusted in length and content. Grading criteria and assessments may be adapted for the individual student. Instructional groupings may vary and activities may be presented in large group, small group, or individually.

A parallel activity is developed. This category includes the use of supplemental materials and activities in which the content is similar or directly related to the curriculum. High interest, low vocabulary texts may be used. At this level, the functional value of the curriculum is determined and activities created are similar or related to the curricular content. These activities include "hands-on" or activity based. At this level, the use of authentic activities and assessments are appropriate.

The classroom activity is the same, but the final outcome is different. In this category, the student performs the same type of activities as their peer group, but the outcome is directly related to the student's goals on the Individualized Education Plan. At this level the student may listen to a class lecture, but the individual goal may be to "sit quietly" for a specific amount of time without interrupting. The student may copy a sentence from the blackboard, but the individual goal is to develop fine motor skills. In math, the student may add or subtract with the calculator, but the student's actual goal is to learn the functions of the calculator. These are functional goals. Functional goals are based on skills the student needs to acquire to live independently as an adult. This independent setting may be a traditional home setting, a supervised apartment or a group home setting.

When adapting material keep considering the following areas:

The Student's Goal: The final outcome may be adjusted. The student may be required to learn the location of regional states on a map instead of both location and capitals. The student may practice letter formation instead of learning to spell a specific list of words.

Level of Difficulty: The student may acquire information through a high interest/low vocabulary text or with the use of supplemental materials. Students may work on basic addition facts instead of more complex addition problems.

Length of Assignment: The number of items the student is expected to learn or complete may be adjusted.

Additional Time: The time allowed to take a test may be increased or the student may be allowed an extra day to complete an assignment.

Input/Output of Information: The student may receive information through cooperative groups or small group instruction, computers, or with the use of visual aids and manipulative materials. The student may share knowledge in ways that replace the traditional paper and pencil assignments. This may include oral presentations, demonstrations, a tape recorder, communication board, computer or with gestures.

Participation in Class Activities: The level at which the student participates in classroom activities may be adjusted. The student's goal may be to participate in the group setting without academic expectations.

Support Systems: The student may receive additional support with paraprofessionals, peer teaching, buddy systems or study halls.

Curriculum Accommodations

The easiest way to illustrate the process of adapting material is to use a hypothetical example. Photocopy Worksheet 18 in the Appendix. Read the following hypothetical example and fill in the worksheet.

John is a 7th grade student with a learning disability. John's ability falls within the average range. He receives special education service in the areas of reading and written language. John's language (both receptive and expressive) is at grade level. John does well in math class and participates in problem solving activities. He actively participants during group discussions and works well in a cooperative group. John consistently does well on lab experiments in Science class.

Step I: Note John's strengths:

* Average ability
* Receptive and expressive language commensurate with the perceived ability
* Strong aptitude for math
* Participates in class
* Works well in cooperative groups
* Does well with hands-on activities
* Enjoys discussion activities

Since this is a hypothetical situation, the list is short. If John was an actual student, the team would be able to elaborate on these strengths.

Step II: Determine the goals for the subject area.

* John will complete 80% of the social studies assignments.
* John will complete the classroom assessments with at least 70% accuracy.

Once Step II is complete, turn to the Table of Contents in this book. This book will save you time, shorten your planning sessions and provide a basis for communication when adapting materials for students with disabilities. First, read through the chapter titles. Determine which chapters are most appropriate for the student. The accommodations have already been compiled for you.

Since John (the hypothetical student) receives support in reading and written language, the following areas were chosen from the Table of Contents:

* Textbook Adaptations
* Creating Audiocassettes
* Daily Assignments

 ❋ Written Language
 ❋ Note Taking
 ❋ Alternate Forms of Assessments

Step III: Brainstorm possible ideas and strategies to help John to compensate for his disability. Some ideas may be:

 ❋ Provide audiocassettes for the materials that are difficult for John to read independently.
 ❋ Use cooperative groups during class. Allow John to work with a partner on written assignments.
 ❋ Provide a study guide for each unit. On the study guide, list the objectives for which John will be held accountable.
 ❋ Provide a partner when lectures require John to take notes. Provide a copy of the notes to John.
 ❋ Written tests should be taken in an individual setting. Allow John to demonstrate knowledge in an alternate form to alleviate long written assignments. Oral presentation for final projects would be appropriate.

Step IV: As a team, decide which ideas to implement. Determine the person responsible to adapt the material (the audiocassette and typing of the study guide could be completed by a volunteer) and the person responsible to implement the idea in the classroom setting. Worksheets #19, #20, and #21 are alternate worksheets that can be used.

When making accommodations, it is important to implement only a few strategies at one time. Worksheet #22 is a Log Sheet that can be used to record and document the results. Be sure to allow ample time for the student to adjust before adding additional strategies or deciding that a specific idea doesn't work. Since all students are unique, a strategy that works for one student will not necessarily work for another.

The strategies in this book are compiled from educators in inclusive settings. There are hundreds from which to choose! These ideas will contribute to the success of all students in inclusive settings!

"Your goal should be out of reach, but not out of sight."

Anita DeFrantz

"A man who removes a mountain begins by removing small stones."

Chinese Proverb

Chapter Three

Textbook Adaptations

"How can Susan be included when she is unable to read the textbook?" Perhaps the question should be rephrased. "How much of the material is Susan able to learn and understand when the information is presented in another manner?" When rephrasing the question, our focus turns toward the student's strength instead of emphasizing the student's weakness.

The majority of the students who receive special education services encounter difficulty with reading. Although the emphasis in this chapter is on accommodations, formalized reading instruction should continue for the student. As a team, it will need to be determined when this will occur. During the elementary day, it may occur when students are grouped for reading or during a time block predetermined at an IEP meeting. At the middle school and secondary level it would be appropriate to incorporate reading into a study skills block or during a study hall period.

There are many commercial reading programs available that may be used to supplement the adopted curriculum. If the adopted reading curriculum emphasizes a phonetic approach, consider supplementing the program with a whole language component. This will help the students with auditory processing difficulties and the students who are visual learners. If the program emphasizes whole language, consider incorporating additional phonics based materials. In reality, some students simply are not ready for a formalized reading program in first grade. For these students, phonemic awareness training may be appropriate. Phonemic awareness is a component of phonics, but it teaches auditory sounds independent of graphic letters. Phonemic awareness training for students can be taught as a prerequisite to reading or used to supplement the reading curriculum. Students who may benefit from phonemic awareness training are student who are unable to hear differences in words such as *pen* and *pin,* who substitute sounds such as *chrain* for *train,* or who have difficulty rhyming words. For students who receive speech and language services, phonemic awareness training could be included into this service.

Although students must continue to receive supplemental reading instruction, textbook accommodations are critical if the student is to experience success throughout the school day.

The ideas listed below are not limited to the reading textbook. Use the following strategies and ideas for Science, Social Studies, English and supplemental textbooks. Whether the student reads the material alone, with support, or listens to a tape, always make sure the student is aware and is held responsible for the follow up activities.

60. Read the text aloud to the class using a guided reading procedure. When reading aloud, frequently provide location clues such as page number and paragraph location. Students who are unable to read the text may listen and look at the pictures. Guided reading also helps the student who tends to daydream during class.

61. Read the text aloud to a small group. The students with disabilities are included in the small group. Vary the groups so students become familiar with small group procedures and become acquainted with other students in their class.

62. Divide the students into two groups. The general education teacher and special education teacher or paraprofessional can read and discuss the information with separate groups. Be sure both teachers have the same outcomes and list of discussion questions. This setting allows all students to actively participate in the class activity.

63. Group students into small cooperative groups and allow students to read aloud. The student with special needs

may not feel comfortable reading aloud at the beginning. As the student's comfort level increases, more risks will be taken.

Choral reading allows all students to actively participate. With choral reading the students read aloud with the teacher or a small group of students read aloud together.

Cloze reading is another option when reading in groups. When using a cloze reading procedure the adult reads aloud and randomly stops, allowing the students fill in the missing words.

64. Provide, in advance, an outline of the material. Allow the student to take notes on the outline while the other students read aloud.

65. Give the student a list of the discussion questions for preview. This helps the student to focus on important material.

Furnish a pad of Post-It™ Notes to the student. The student may jot down notes, vocabulary words, or questions about the material. These notes can be applied directly to the textbook for easy reference.

66. Record the lesson. Allow the student to listen to the tape in a small group or with a peer. (See the section titled Creating Audiocassettes.) Color-code a master textbook to accompany the audiocassette. Highlight the important information that the student is expected to learn: vocabulary words and their definitions; important facts; and specific material covered on the assessment. Tape a corresponding color key in the front of the textbook. The text is now individualized for the specific course.

67. Tape record alternate pages of the textbook. Allow the student to listen to one page and then read one either silently or aloud. This helps the student who is struggling to keep the same pace as his or her peers. You may also

want to include a color-coded textbook as described in #66.

68.   Paraphrase textbook material on tape. Include only the most important material. Paraphrasing is difficult. You must be very familiar with the material before attempting to do this, or the paraphrased version may become longer than the text version!

69.   Preview and discuss the pictures, diagrams and charts with the student before reading. The student is better able to rely on visual clues and has background information on which to build upon.

70.   Contact the textbook publisher. Often publishers have adapted materials and supplemental textbooks that correlate to the grade level textbooks.

Novels and Free Choice Reading

71.   Ask students to tape record their favorite books. This activity can be assigned as a project or extra credit activity. Students reading below grade level can record books for younger students. Students may check out the books individually or as a small group from the classroom library or the media center. For nonreaders, these tapes may be used during silent reading time.

Note: Check the school library to see if they have books, novels, and disability awareness titles. If not, you may want to recommend a list of titles for purchase.

72.   While reading textbooks out loud, simultaneously record the material. With textbook material, students can use this tape for chapter review as it includes both student questions and discussion points. When reading novels, these tapes can be used in a classroom library. Students

may check out the book and tape to reread or listen to at a later time.

73. For nonreaders, ask the paraprofessional, a volunteer, or peer to read aloud to the student. Include other students in the group. Elementary students love listening to stories. At the secondary level, select students to read aloud to others.

74. Popular novels and stories are often available on video. Furnish the student with a video to view before reading. Be sure to preview it first! The video will help the student establish the storyline, develop the characters and build some background before reading. Oftentimes there are major differences between the video and the author's written work. If this is the case, include a group activity where students compare and contrast the differences between the written and visual presentation of the material.

75. Appoint a student to be the *Teacher of the Day*. This student can read aloud to a small group of students or to an individual student.

76. Provide a collection of novels and short stories on audiocassettes for students. Include the books from ideas #71-75 and add some of the classics. Check with local organizations for learning disabilities and services for the blind. They may have prerecorded materials available.

77. Choose high interest/low vocabulary level books. Many publishers have chapter books available for purchase in this format.

Previewing and Preteaching Strategies for Texts

Many students experience success with the curriculum when allowed to preview the materials before the lesson is actually presented. Previewing and preteaching strategies can be completed with the general or special education teacher, the paraprofessional, or at home as a homework assignment. These straightforward techniques produce marvelous results for some students.

78. Allow the student to take home an audiocassette of the material before it is read in class. This will allow the student to become familiar with the main characters, the story, and plot.

79. Provide extra time for the student to preview and discuss the photos, illustrations, captions, headings, and chapter questions with an adult. This helps to build background information. Relate the new concepts to previously learned concepts.

80. Preview bold-faced print and italicized words, headings and subheadings with the student. Read and define the words in the context presented in the textbook.

81. Furnish a weekly list of both vocabulary and boldface type words to the student in advance. Use the words in sentences directly related to the context of the text, instead of isolation to avoid double meanings. The student can preview or study the vocabulary at home.

82. Generate chapter vocabulary lists for textbooks. Once again include only the definitions relevant to the textbook. Place this information into packets. Don't forget to include the chapter title and page numbers as a heading. The students may use this material at home to assist with their homework assignments, unit previews, and test reviews.

83. Offer vocabulary lists from classroom textbooks to speech and language teachers. This helps coordinate the language services into the curriculum and provides additional support to the student.

84. Provide a list of discussion questions and ask the student to find the answers. Include page number location clues.

85. Purchase several additional textbooks specifically for the purpose of highlighting important information. Color code the student textbook. An example would be to use yellow for the vocabulary words, blue for the definitions, and green to highlight topic sentences, facts and important information. If it is not possible to purchase or highlight within the text, photocopy or scan the relevant information for the student. The student will be able to write on the copy. If you are scanning large amounts of textbook material, call the publisher to request permission before copying. Often publishers have both hardcover and consumable versions available. The consumable books often are less expensive.

86. Provide an outline of the main ideas and vocabulary words for each unit. After reading the main ideas and vocabulary words ask the student to answer the following questions. What do I already know about the topic? How to the words relate to the topic? What would I like to learn about the topic?

87. Paraphrasing is helpful for most students. It also helps the teacher know whether or not the student has grasped the concept. To assist with paraphrasing, ask the student to read a section. When complete ask the student to state the main idea in their own words and the share two or three supporting details. Some students find that paraphrasing the material into a tape recorder is helpful, especially when reviewing for tests.

88. Offer a set of textbooks for home use. Before taking the text home, explain how to locate main ideas, key words,

detail in sentences and how to use the glossary and appendix.

Creating Audiocassettes

Audiocassettes are a wonderful tool for many students with disabilities. They may be used during the day or at home. Audiocassettes also provide support to the student who has been absent. If the goal is simply to listen to the material in place of reading, contact the publisher and ask if the book is available on audiocassette. Audiocassettes need to be created if you would like the material paraphrased, partial text such as every other page, or only the material that focuses on the specific objectives of the individual class. Creating audiocassettes is time consuming. Once the initial cassettes are recorded, be sure to make additional copies for grade levels or departments. Keep the original in a safe place.

89. Use the many sources of volunteers available: parents, peers, older students, community group members, drama club members, or honor society members to assist when making audiocassettes. Make additional copies, label and file for future use.

90. When enlisting volunteers to record audiocassettes, carefully examine the reading quality and reading rate of the volunteer before the tapes are made. If the reader speaks too rapidly the student will not be able to follow along. If the reader reads too slowly, the student may not grasp the main idea or worse yet, fall asleep.

91. When preparing audiocassettes, have the speaker read in a clear voice. Texts should be read at 120-175 words per minute. Eliminate background noise. Doors slamming, telephones ringing, and muffled voices often are sound effects that do not correspond with the textbook materials. These sounds often distract the student.

92. Begin the audiocassette with a statement of the title, the chapter, and the section or the pages recorded on the tape. Use a consistent labeling system for easy filing.

93. Include study guidelines at the beginning to orient the student to the main points of the section.

94. Include comprehension checkpoints on the tape such as; *"Please stop the tape here and list three uses of water."* When the tape resumes, provide the answer. This helps the student be actively involved with the lesson.

95. Provide special textbooks that correspond to the tape. Place a symbol key in the text that relates to specific portions of the audiocassette. For example, an asterisk may indicate a portion of the text that has been paraphrased on the audiocassette. A stop sign may indicate that the student should stop and provide the definition for a word in bold type. Devise your own system.

96. For older students, coordinate the cassette with anticipated assessment questions. At strategic points, ask the student to stop the tape and summarize the information, state the main idea of the paragraph or define the bold faced vocabulary words which will appear on the assessment. When the tape restarts, provide the answer to the question.

97. Provide students with an outline of important material to use as a guide when listening to materials. The student can add additional information to the outline.

98. If discussion questions are included at the end of the audiocassette, provide page number location clues or include the answers on the audiocassette so the student may immediately self-check the response.

99. Paraphrase the entire text, with simplified vocabulary for students who are unable to read. Relate the information to the visuals presented in the textbook.

Tracking Difficulties

Have you ever worked with a student who is continually losing the place in the textbook? You may feel as though you are always redirecting the student. If this occurs the student is probably experiencing difficulty with visual tracking.

100. Partner the student with a peer and allow the peer to assist the student with visual tracking. Allow students to share a textbook.

101. Give specific instruction as to where the student should begin reading.

102. Provide frequent oral location clues (page and paragraph numbers) when reading aloud. Redirect the student by pointing out page and paragraph numbers frequently.

103. Seat the student near the teacher so tracking can be easily monitored. Check frequently to see if the student is in the correct location.

104. Use a bookmark to help the student keep his or her place.

105. Place a horizontal arrow running from the left to the right side of an index card. This will aid the student with directionality.

106. Cut a window into an index card. This helps the student focus because the student can only see a few lines or small area.

107. Provide a picture frame made from construction paper for the student. The student will be able to see several lines of print, yet will be able to block out distracting stimuli.

108. Allow the student to listen to the material and view the pictures while someone else reads the text aloud.

Hearing Impairments

If there is a student with a mild or severe hearing loss in the classroom, frequently a specialist or consultant of the hearing impaired will provide materials and suggestions to both the general and special educator. If a student has a severe hearing loss, a sign language interpreter is often available to help the student. The specialist provides direct service to the student and supplemental materials to the general and special education teacher. The following suggestions provide additional support for the student with a hearing impairment.

109. Seat the student near the teacher.

110. Always use visual signals to secure the student's attention when reading aloud.

111. Speak and read clearly in a normal tone and at a moderate pace.

112. Rephrase content areas or questions to make the lesson more easily understood.

113. Provide the student with an outline and vocabulary lists before introducing new material. Encourage the student to preview the information at home before the lesson is presented.

114. Repeat and summarize information when presented orally.

115. Present vocabulary words in sentences. Many words look similar to lip readers.

116. If the student reads lips, provide the student with a swivel chair, so student will be able to see the teacher and the interpreter at all times.

Vision Impairments

If a student with a visual impairment is in the classroom, you will consult frequently with a teacher of the visually impaired. This specialist will provide materials and offer suggestions. Oftentimes enlarged materials are used. If this is the case, additional storage space will be needed as these materials often will not fit on a traditional bookshelf.

It is important to note that if the student with visual impairments appears to be inattentive or looking around in the classroom, the student may be relying on auditory skills to gain information. Students with visual impairments often experience visual fatigue during classroom assignments.

117. Order specialized materials, such as enlarged textbooks, magnifiers, closed circuit television and computer software with enlarged fonts and pictures. Another option is to scan and enlarge the material for the student.

118. Provide audiocassettes for the student's textbooks. Create audiocassettes on cassette players with variable recording speeds. This will allow the student to increase the speed as the auditory skills become more refined. Contact the local Society for the Blind and become aware of the services they have to offer.

119. Allow extra time for assignment completion. Be aware of visual fatigue that often occurs during activities requiring continuous use of visual skills. Some of the signs of visual fatigue may include: red eyes; rubbing of the eyes; laying the head on the desk; and squinting.

120. Minimize fatigue by modifying the number and length of the activities when visual concentration is required. Always remember the objective of the lesson. If a student is able to listen to the information, or demonstrate knowledge in an alternate format, allow the student to do so.

121. When addressing the student, be sure to verbally call the student by name. Often the student will not see the visual clues.

122. Tape record assignments so the student may replay it as often as needed.

123. When using Braille or new supplemental devices in the classroom, provide training for the entire class, when appropriate. Show students how to write their names or label various objects in the classroom with Braille. Allow students to try the magnifiers and experiment with the computer programs. The students will be excited by the newly acquired knowledge and it becomes a learning experience for all students.

124. Touch is important for visually impaired students. Provide hands-on experiences whenever possible.

"Success is the maximum utilization of the ability you have."

Zig Zigler

FRANK LEARNS THAT INCLUSION DOESN'T HAVE TO BE ROCKET SCIENCE.

Source: "Ants in His Pants: Absurdities and Realities of Special Education"
by Michael F. Giangreco © 1998 Reprinted with permission.

This page may not be reproduced

"Limitations live only in our minds. But if we use our imaginations, our possibilities become limitless."

Jamie Paolinetti

Chapter Four

Daily Assignments

Whenever a daily assignment is given, the purpose of the assignment should be determined. The majority of daily assignments are used to verify the student's understanding of the concept presented. Although it is customary to ask the student to respond in a written format, this is not always possible for students with disabilities. Some students are overwhelmed which results in frustration and acting out on the part of the student. If this is the case, the assignment may need to be adapted to meet the needs of the student. Always determine the outcome and then adapt the assignment according to the student's needs.

An important question that arises when discussing inclusive education is "How will the student receive remedial support when the student is included in the classroom the entire day?" When students are working on daily assignments, it is an optimum time for the student to receive direct instruction from the special education teacher or reteaching from the paraprofessional. Often daily seatwork activities are designed to reinforce previously taught skills or to check for understanding of a specific skill. Determine the appropriateness of the activity. Ask, "Is this beneficial to the student?" and "Is it important for the student to complete the entire assignment?" If not, use the time to provide a supplemental series or to reinforce previously taught skills. If there are additional students in the classroom who may benefit from reteaching or reinforcement, consider including these students in the group. Additional ideas for adaptations of daily assignments may also be found under the specific subject areas.

125. Divide the assignment in half. Allow the student to complete only even or odd problems. If the student is able to demonstrate mastery by completing only a portion of the assignment, allow the student to work on other assignments where additional time is needed.

126. Break the assignment into segments and allow the student to complete the assignment over a period of several days.

127. Use a cover sheet for long assignments. Oftentimes a long assignment seems so overwhelming the student feels frustrated before beginning.

128. Use cooperative groups or pair the students. One student can read aloud while another student writes the response. All students can participate fully within the group.

129. Allow the student to answer verbally into a tape recorder. This works especially well for the student who has difficulty with fine motor, but is able to read and understand the material.

130. If the assignment permits, provide the student with a photocopy. Allow the student to highlight, underline, or fill in the blank on the copy instead of copying the entire paragraph, list of sentences, or the page of math problems.

131. Provide an assignment sheet to help the student organize and prioritize daily assignments. Include due dates. Be sure the student understands the difference between *do* and *due*! If parents are participating with a home/school assignment book, it is important the student also has the correct spelling of these two words.

132. Rewrite materials at an appropriate reading level or provide a parallel activity for the same skill.

133. Permit a partner to write the student's response.

134. Allow the student to respond orally. Oftentimes, material can be summarized and related questions answered within several minutes. By permitting the student to complete some assignments orally, the student has more time to produce a quality assignment with the remainder of the daily assignments. This is appropriate for the student who is continually behind the class with daily assignments.

135. Provide additional drill and practice sessions for the student. Work towards mastery of the skill. Monitor and adjust the final outcome if necessary.

136. Allow additional time for completion of assignments. The student may not be able to complete the entire assignment during one class period.

137. Let the student illustrate the answer instead of responding in a written format.

138. Create supplementary materials that coincide with the text at an easier readability level. Many teachers' guides include blackline masters for various levels. Often supplemental materials developed for the English as a Second Language student are appropriate for the student with special needs.

139. Provide parallel activities at an appropriate level. For example, if the objective is to locate nouns, use the student's reading text and ask the student to write the nouns from the story. If the student is unable to read, have the student locate objects in the classroom that are nouns.

140. Develop written contracts for curriculum units. This allows the length or assignments to be modified simply by highlighting the assignment the student must complete.

141. Supply the student with a package of Post-It™ notes. The student can write incomplete assignments on a separate note. When the assignment is completed, the student throws the note away. If the assignment is not completed

during the school day, the student places the note in the assignment book at the end of the class.

142. Allow the student to use a computer, word processor or calculator to complete required work.

"The impossible is often the untried."

Jim Goodman

"Rough diamonds may sometimes be mistaken for worthless pebbles."

Sir Thomas Browne

Chapter Five

Written Language

Written language incorporates a wide range of skills. Students may experience difficulty for a variety of reasons. Some students are unable to transfer their ideas into a written format. Others have trouble with the grammar, syntax or the mechanics. A third group may experience difficulty due to language limitations or the ability to process language.

For some students, writing is so laborious, you may need to bypass the writing process altogether. For this student, the mode of output often will be different than the other students in the class. In this situation, the student may need a "buddy" to take notes or transcribe answers, projects may need to be presented orally, taped recorded or perhaps videotaped, and written exams may need to be followed up with a short oral exam or interview.

Generating Ideas

"I have a student who simply refuses to write," or "I have a student sits and just stares at the paper. The student refuses to even attempt to write." These concerns are heard frequently among educators. There may be times when a student is so frustrated with writing, and language processing is so difficult, they simply refuse to write.

143. The student with special needs should be encouraged to write on a daily basis. Journaling is a form of writing that can be completed daily. A free response, question/answer format, or asking the student to respond to special event often will encourage the student to write.

144. Provide specific instructions for the assignment. Write a sentence or two to help the student get started. Gradually decrease the structure as the student becomes more confident in their ability to write.

145. If a student has difficulty generating ideas, create a student/teacher journal. With a student/teacher journal, the teacher is able to direct specific questions to the individual student. The student responds to the questions in a written format. Questions can be tailored toward the student's specific interests.

146. Ask the student to choose a familiar topic. Generate a word bank and allow the student to write about the same topic for several days. Another option is to assemble a small group to work with the student. Ask the group to spend 3-5 minutes brainstorming the topic. Provide the word bank to all students in the group. The students may help one another with the structure, grammar and spelling. Vary the group of students.

147. When the student is able to generate ideas, help the student develop an outline of the story or topic. The student is able to follow the outline to sequence their thoughts and organize the ideas.

148. Keep a box of old photographs, pictures from magazines, and animal or nature pictures in the classroom. Ask the student to select a picture and spend several minutes listing descriptive words to describe the picture.

149. If the student has difficulty generating ideas, select a topic together. Request the student to write a minimum amount

daily. (You may have to start at one sentence!) Build on the topic each day. The next week increase the goal. Make sure the student is held responsible to meet their individual goal.

150. Ask the student bring a photograph from home. It may be a picture of a vacation, party, an important event, or an important person in their life. Since the student has background information about the photo, often it is easier for the student to write about it.

151. If the student is unable to write a sentence, write descriptive words or illustrate the idea. The words may be combined into simple sentences at a later time.

 For those who are unable to write, provide old magazines. The student can look for pictures related to a specific topic. Glue the pictures onto construction paper. Topics can be varied depending upon the ability level of the student. Simple topics may include pictures related to food, clothing, colors, or plants. More complex topics may include pictures related to the weather, products made of wood, items that require electricity to run, or mammals. Later, the student can copy or list the words that correspond to the picture.

152. Ask the Speech/Language teacher for sequence cards. Ask the student to write a sentence about each step. If this is too difficult ask the student to write a sentence for the last step only. The following day, ask the student to write about the next to last and last step. Proceed until all cards have been used.

153. Ask the paraprofessional to write the student's ideas and the student may copy the idea or story from the model.

154. If the student is unable to write, the paraprofessional or another adult can write the student's response. The student may trace the response with multicolored pencils, crayons

or fine tipped markers. For motivation add variety to the student assignment. Vary the size, shape, texture and color of the paper, or use a small chalkboard.

The Writing Process

Written language is difficult for many students in the classroom, but especially for those with special needs. Spelling, grammar, mechanics, organization, punctuation, incomplete and run on sentences, sequence, subject-verb agreement are only a few of the complexities incorporated into a sentence, paragraph and short story. Students need direct instruction and a great deal of guided practice to become proficient writers.

Post reference charts and various lists throughout the classroom as reminders. Some examples of helpful charts and lists include: manuscript and cursive alphabets, commonly misspelled words, writing process steps (prewriting, composition, response, revise, edit, and final product), transition words, capitalization words, abbreviations, contractions, and a model of the expected standards for written assignments required on daily assignments.

155. Avoid excessive corrections in the mechanical aspects of writing so the student does not become discouraged with the process. Place the emphasis on the development of the ideas rather than the mechanics of writing.

    When placing emphasis on the mechanics and spelling, many students will play safe: some will not experiment with new words, others will write far less for fear of making mistakes, and still other students will not write anything.

156. Help students organize their ideas before writing.

    Demonstrate how to use mapping skills. A "map" should include the key ideas and words for the main topic. Mapping helps the student to visualize the relationship between the topic and the paragraphs of the story. A "map" is simple to create. To illustrate, the topic of "Dogs" will be used. In the center of an 8 ½" x 11" paper write the word DOG. Now fold the paper into quarter sections. In each of the four sections a word is written that pertains to some aspect of the DOG. Subtopics may include: feeding, exercising, grooming and training. In each of the four sections list words and phrases that pertain to the individual subtopic. When the mapping exercise is complete, the student creates an introduction, uses the four individual subtopics to write the paragraphs and adds a closing paragraph. The story is completely organized for the student.

Venn diagrams are frequently used to compare and contrast two or more characters, people or events. To create a simple Venn diagram, the student draws two large overlapping circles in the center of the paper. The similarities between the two topics are placed in the space where the two circles overlap. The student uses the outside portion of each circle to list the contrasting information. Once again, this helps students to organize the information in a simple way. To compare three stories or events, three circles may be used. Use 11" x 17" paper when comparing more than two so there is ample room to write!

Charts are also used to compare and contrast ideas. Use one column to list the similarities and another to list the differences.

Story maps can be used. After reading a story or novel, list the critical elements of the story: setting, characters, problem or event, the action, and the resolution.

157. Prepare students to write. Before writing a story ask students answer the following questions to help formulate an organized storyline:

   * Who is the main character?
   * Who else is in the story?

 ❊ What does the main character want to do in the story?
 ❊ What happens when the main character does this?
 ❊ How does the story end?

These simple questions help students to organize their thoughts and develop the basic outline for the story.

158. Explain the importance of a beginning, middle and end in each paragraph. Incorporate transition words such as *first, next, then, last* or *finally* when writing paragraphs. It helps the student sequence their thoughts.

 Practice the use of transition words by asking students to teach a peer or small group "how-to" do something. At the elementary level it may be as simple as how to make a sandwich, lace a pair of tennis shoes, or introduce an adult. At the secondary level, the student may want to share an area of expertise such as how to shoot a basket, apply makeup, set a table correctly, or use a video camera.

159. Teach students to proofread and edit their own work. Provide a simple proofreading checklist for individual assignments or post a proofreading checklist on a wall chart. An individual checklist, works well, as it can be adapted to the IEP goals. Depending upon the student's grade level and goals, some or all of the following may be included: capitalization, punctuation, misspelled words, margins, paragraph indentation and sentence sense, and descriptive words. Whether using an individual chart or a classroom chart, the student should read the entire paper and edit the paper for one item at a time. If using the above list, the student would read the entire paper and edit the paper for capital letters. When completed, it is crossed off on the individual form. The second time, the student reads the paper and edits the punctuation only. The student continues until the entire paper is corrected. When complete, the student may be required to add a specific number of descriptive words to the story.

Periodically, edit a story as a group. Make a transparency of a class story (name omitted) or create your own. Practice editing the story on the overhead.

160. The SPACE strategy may be used as an error monitoring strategy when writing. The acronym SPACE stands for the following:

   * SPELLING
   * PUNCTUATION
   * APPEARANCE
   * CAPITALIZATION
   * ERROR ANALYISIS

161. To help with neatness and legibility, incorporate real-life situations into the writing experience. Pen pals, thank you notes, job applications and writing checks are all examples of real life situations where neatness and legibility are very important.

162. Ask the student to read the story aloud or record it when complete. Ask the student to pause after each sentence. Many students will be able to detect run-on sentences and grammatical errors. Allow the student ample time to make the corrections to their papers.

163. Since written language is a form of communication, allow the students to share their stories and reports often. It is important for students to see and hear good models. Do not require students to read in front of the class if they do not desire to do so.

164. Allow students to use a word processing program for final edit copies. Students can conduct a final spell and grammar check.

165. For some students you may need to look at the quality of the assignment instead of the quantity. When working on topic sentences, details, and a closing sentence, allow the

student to produce one quality paragraph instead of a series of paragraphs.

166. When working on class reports, allow the student to use a fill in the blank form. An example for the topic Birds might be:

> *My bird is a* _____. *He lives in the* _____ *part of the United States. He is* _____ *in color.*

The student can add as many details as necessary. This procedure may be adapted for students at all grade levels.

167. When writing research papers, assist the student with the formulation of the topic sentence. Encourage the student to look for details. For elementary students, begin with one topic sentence and several supporting detail sentences. At the secondary level you may have five to ten topic sentences, depending upon the subject and the class requirements. For some students, modify the number of sources required in the bibliography, especially if the student has difficulty reading.

168. Allow the student to present the final project in another format. A videotape, demonstration, display or oral presentation may capitalize on the student's strengths.

Prewriting Stage

With some students, there is a large discrepancy between the student's ability to write and the writing ability of their peer group. Some students may be in a prewriting stage. If the student is in a prewriting stage, parallel or supplemental activities can be provided according to the student's Individualized Education Plan. The ideas and strategies listed in the *Fine Motor* section will provide additional support for these students.

169. Allow the student to dictate the story to you, while an adult writes. The student can practice reading the story aloud and tracing the letters of individual words.

170. Use the student's personal vocabulary and combine reading, written language and spelling! Ask the student to dictate a simple story while an adult writes. Divide the story into individual sentences. The student then copies one sentence onto each individual sentence strip. The sentence strips can later be organized into the final story. Sentence strips work well as the daily goal can easily be easily monitored and adjusted. When the story is complete the student can practice reading the story. By rearranging the strips, you will be able to note whether the student is reading or has simply memorized the story. This often helps students learn to read and spell simple words. Once the student is familiar with the story, create an audiocassette. The student can listen and practice reading aloud with the tape. The words from the story can also be incorporated into a spelling list.

171. Purchase commercial paper with raised lines so the student is able to practice letter and word formation. If you are at a secondary level, contact primary level teachers to see what is available.

172. Write a question and the student's response in pencil. Allow the student to trace their response with a felt tip pen and then illustrate. Use colored pencils for multiple tracings.

173. Practice copying material from the board, the overhead or from a close model onto paper. The student's final outcome may be different than the outcome of the peer group. In this situation the outcome may be a handwriting goal whereas the other students may be required to complete an assignment with the material.

174. In place of writing the response, ask the student to illustrate it.

175. Trace templates to develop fine motor control. Both letter and picture templates are available.

176. Use tracing paper and have the student trace large objects from a coloring book.

177. Have the student reproduce simple shapes from a model. Begin with bold line shapes and move into connecting dots and lines.

178. Use the time to practice letter formation. Use clay, sand trays and tracers. For some students, prompts are needed. If a paraprofessional or adult volunteer is available, they may need to give verbal prompts or gently guide the student's hand during the initial stages.

179. Allow the student to work on dot-to-dot pictures. Use both A,B,C and 1,2,3 pictures.

180. Use the time for additional fine motor development activities such as stringing beads, pegboard designs, sewing cards, weaving, cutting or clay.

Spelling Difficulties

Spelling is difficult for many adults. Imagine the difficulties many students encounter! Set a positive example for students by frequently looking up unknown words in the dictionary. Also demonstrate the use of a thesaurus. A collection of resources and reference aids should be available in the classroom. If possible, include several levels of both a dictionary and a thesaurus. Provide students with a list of commonly misspelled words. Teach students how to use both the grammar and spell check on the computer.

181. At first glance, a paper with numerous spelling errors appears to lack creativity or contain solid ideas. Allow the

student to spell phonetically. Have the student read the paper to you if necessary. Revise the paper with the student. Give encouragement to all attempts.

182. Ask students to keep a personal list of commonly misspelled words. Each time a student asks how to spell a word, or looks it up in a reference book, ask the student to list it in their individual dictionary. Most students continually misspell the same words and soon they will see the pattern.

183. Allow the student to tape record the response and transcribe it at a later time. Encourage the student to use a dictionary and a thesaurus.

Fine Motor Difficulty

Some students have wonderful ideas and are very creative. A delay in fine motor skills often causes difficulty and frustration for the student when transferring the ideas to paper. Instead of allowing the creativity to flow, the student may write in short, choppy sentences to compensate for the difficulty in fine motor control. Interestingly, when the obstacle of writing is removed, these students may become some of your most creative students.

184. Check the student's pencil grip. Place adhesive tape or a pencil grip on the pencil. If the paper frequently moves on the desk, tape the paper in place. For older students, a clipboard often helps keep the paper in place.

185. Provide various sizes of wide ruled paper. Begin with the large rule paper size and slowly decrease the line size until the student is able to use grade appropriate paper. If the correct size of paper is unavailable commercially, create the appropriate size either manually or on the computer. Photocopy it.

186. Write the student's answer or story in pencil and allow the student to trace it with a fine tip marker or colored pencils. For final copies, encourage students to use erasable pens.

187. Provide a close-up model for the student to copy instead of copying from a distant model such as the board or overhead. If an older student struggles with cursive writing, allow the student to print or use a laptop computer.

188. Give the student a small alphabet card so they can see the correct formation of the letters. Allow either manuscript or cursive, depending on the student's preference.

189. If appropriate, write some or all of the assignment for the student. The parents should be made aware of the expectations regarding homework assignments. Indicate under which circumstances the homework assignment may be hand written or typed for the student.

190. Modify the length of the assignment. If the assignment is long, break it into sections and allow the student to complete one section at a time. A long assignment may take several days for completion.

191. Look at the quality, instead of the quantity produced. When completing a quality assignment, make sure the student has ample time to complete the final product.

192. Provide the student with a word processor or a lap top computer to use with long assignments.

"Educational progress depends on the ability of the teacher to perceive the untapped resources of the student and to develop techniques of using these resources to the best advantage."

Rudolf Dreikurs

What I hear, I forget; what I see, I remember; what I do, I understand.

Chinese Proverb

Chapter Six

Spelling

Spelling words should be compatible with the reading level of the student. Accommodations for spelling programs may be as simple as adapting the length of the list or they may be complex, such as creating an appropriate spelling program.

For the student who is not yet ready for a formalized spelling program, use the time to develop fine motor skills and sound association. For some students, phonemic awareness training may be appropriate to help develop sensitivity to the sound structures of the spoken word. When students understand the sound structure and are able to manipulate the sound segments they will then be able to make a gradual transition into a spelling program.

For students who understand the sound symbol relationship teach the consonants first, as there are only a few exceptions to the rules. Develop picture clues for the vowel sounds and post these charts in the room. Make sure you consistently refer to the same pictures when working with the vowel sounds. Once the student has developed the sound/symbol relationships, word families may be taught. Reinforce word families with students. When the response is automatic, move on to the next word family.

In the Study Methods section of this chapter, various study methods are listed.

Grade Level Spelling Lists

Often students with disabilities can succeed in the regular spelling curriculum with minimal adaptations.

193. Modify the spelling list by adjusting the number of items on the list.

194. Set individual spelling goals. For the student who continually fails spelling tests, the goal may be to master only two words the first week. The goal is then increased after the student has experienced success at the beginning level. If a student has continually experienced failure, it is unrealistic to expect the student to increase the spelling goal from 0% to 100% in one week.

195. Increase the number of words when the student reaches mastery level on three consecutive tests.

196. Group the spelling words into word families so the student is able to focus on the pattern. Once the student understands simple word families such as *at, hat, pat, rat,* change the vowel short vowel. *Hat, pat* and *sat* now become *hot, pot* and *rot.* Make flashcards for individual letters. Use one color for consonants and one for vowels. The students can create their own words.

197. If the student is unable to read a large number of the words on the list, delete the unfamiliar words. Insert commonly used sight words or words that follow the current word patterns.

Creating Spelling Lists

198. When creating supplemental spelling lists, the list should be consistent with the student's reading level. Incorporate

words from the student's basal reader when creating a supplemental spelling program.

199. Choose spelling words that are relevant to the curriculum and consistent with the student's vocabulary. For some students the expectation for the challenge words may be to read the words only.

200. Select a word bank from the student's basal reader. Group the words according to word families. Include several sight words. You may also want to select several bonus words from the reading.

201. Create three separate spelling lists on the computer. One list should be the list used in the classroom setting. The three lists should include: a list on phonetic words; a list of sight words; and a list of both phonetic and sight words. All students can do the same practice exercises as their peers even though the individual list may contain different words. This should help meet the needs of all students in the classroom.

202. Use the previous year's spelling list and adapt it to the format of the current grade level list.

Parallel Spelling Activities

Not all students are ready for a formalized spelling program. Some students may need parallel activities. These activities may be completed alone, with a peer or with the paraprofessional.

203. If a volunteer or paraprofessional is available to work with the student, spend 15 to 20 minutes teaching sound association (phonemic awareness). Emphasize the sounds at the beginning, middle and end of the word. Use pictures in place of letters to represent the sounds. For example show the student three pictures: cat, apple,

napkin. Ask the student to say the first sound of each picture. C A N. Then ask the student to blend the sounds together to make a new word. In this example the word is "can". Using the same three pictures ask the student to tell you how many sounds they hear (3). Ask the student to show you the position of the "c" sound (beginning), the "a" sound (middle), and the "n" sound (end). Once mastered with multiple words, begin to change the initial and ending sounds. When the student has mastered this step you may begin to work with word patterns, which is a prerequisite to rhyming.

When the student is able to apply these skills at the sound level, the student is ready to move to the next level - the relationship between sounds and graphic letters.

Once the student understands the sound relationships in words, begin to relate the sounds to actual letters. When the weekly spelling list is given to the class, as the student can write the first letter of the word on the sheet. The student's goal would be sound association and fine motor development.

204. Provide the student with a selection of individual consonant sounds on index cards. When the word is given to the entire class, the student selects the appropriate initial consonant flash card and holds it up. Once the student learns the initial sounds, this method can be used for ending sounds.

If working on only the sound relationship, the student would have a selection of picture cards and hold up the picture card that relates to the actual sound heard.

205. Begin with basic sight words and simple phonetic words such as a, at, am and an as soon as the student knows several letters and sounds.

206. Begin by associating familiar words with spelling. The student's proper name along with the names of family

members, friends, peers or pets may be appropriate. Use the spelling list to create simple sentences. Practice the sentence until mastery has been reached. This lesson may be incorporated into spelling, handwriting or used as a written language activity. An example would be:

<u>List</u>
I
Meg
am
is
name

I am Meg.
Meg is my name.
My name is Meg.

207. Provide the student with practice pages of the words and sentences. The student may trace the words or sentences with multiple colors of crayons, felt tipped pens or colored pencils. The student can also practice writing the words with a paintbrush and water on a small chalkboard, paint, or shaving cream. Letters and short words can also be written into 8 ½" x 12" pan filled with colored rice, sand or salt.

208. Purchase small 1" tiles (or make your own from tag board) and write the letters from the spelling words on tiles. Write the consonants in one color and vowels in another. Have the student make words with the tiles. Use peers to drill and monitor the student's progress.

Drill and Practice

Drill and practice activities take place daily in the classroom. Vary the assignments. Make sure the student is held accountable for meeting the daily goals.

209. Group the word lists into word families. For example: make, bake and take. Add prefixes to the words such as *re* for remake, retake, rebake. Then add suffixes such as *ing* remaking, retaking, rebaking.

210. Group the words that contain the same prefixes and suffixes to teach patterns. Teach the spelling and meaning of the suffixes and prefixes in isolation. This is especially helps middle and secondary students who no longer have formalized spelling programs.

211. Provide highlighters so students can highlight base words, suffixes and prefixes to aid with visual discrimination. Another option is to ask the students to write each syllable with a different color marker.

212. Teach only one spelling rule at a time.

213. Provide the student with a close up model from which to work. Many students experience difficulty when copying unknown words from a distant model.

214. Combine spelling and handwriting goals to allow time for additional drill and practice.

215. When assigning drill and practice activities for spelling, allow a minimum of ten minutes. Students who experience difficulty with organizational skills will need at least ten minutes to find and organize their materials and then practice the activity.

216. Do not require students to practice all of the words on a daily basis. It may be too overwhelming. Allow the student to practice two or three words per day if the student is frustrated by a long list.

217. Provide a list of drill and practice exercises. Once or twice a week allow the student to choose an additional way to practice the spelling list. Some suggestions of activities include:

Spelling Bingo – each student creates their own card and students may play with a partner or small group during practice time.

Hangman – students play in partners during practice time

Word Finds – students create individual word finds on graph paper and share with a friend.

Poems, Stories, Riddles and Jokes – students create short stories, poems, riddles and jokes with their words to share with others in the class.

Pictures – draw silly pictures and include pictures of the words in the illustrations.

Synonyms, Antonyms, and Homonyms – students select synonyms, antonyms or homonyms corresponding to the spelling list and a peer tries to guess the related spelling word.

Spelling Group Games – if using spelling games such as Spelling Baseball or Spell Downs, be sure students are allowed to use their own learning style. Not all students can spell the words aloud. Allow students to use paper and pencil to write the word before demonstrating their response.

Computers – there are several commercial software programs available in which weekly spelling words may be inserted.

218. Vary the daily drill and practice exercises. Along with paper and pencil tasks, allow the student to practice on the chalkboard, in small groups, or do it orally on tape.

219. For younger students, practice with shaving cream, sand trays, paints or write the words in pudding.

220. Provide the student with an audiocassette of the word list. The student can practice alone during extra class time or take the tape home. This audiocassette may also be used if a student needs to retest or was absent during the test. If a pretest is given to students at the beginning of the week, turn on the tape recorder. The list is then recorded for students who would like to practice with the tape, for those who were absent, and to use if needed for a final test.

221. Provide word strips for the student to trace with crayon or marker. This will provide drill and practice for correct letter formation. Trace each word with three or four colors.

222. Encourage the student to verbalize the sounds while writing the words.

223. Allow the student to practice on a typewriter, computer or word processor. Have the student type each word at least three times. Old manual typewriters can be put to good use for practice.

224. Help students use mnemonic devices. For more difficult words, students can create simple sentences to help them to remember words. For example, for the word *because* a silly sentence may be: *B*rave *E*ddie *C*atches *A*nd *U*ses *S*limy *E*els to fish. For frequently misspelled words ask the students to create silly sentences to share.

Configuration clues often help students to recall the correct spelling. For example, the configuration of the word "because" would include one tall box at the beginning, followed by six small boxes. A common mistake often made when spelling the word "because" is the insertion of the letter k. Since there is only one tall letter, configuration clues help students to remember it is a c rather than a k. The five small boxes will help the student to remember the "cause" part of the word instead of the many variations (cuz, cuse, and cuze) often used.

225. Allow students to experiment and select the study method that works best for them. See next section.

Study Methods for Spelling

For students with disabilities, the most effective method is the method that will capitalize on the student's strengths. Three guidelines for studying spelling are listed here. Allow students to experiment with the various methods to determine which best meets their learning style.

Visual Learners

226. This method focuses on the student's visual strength. This method may be appropriate for students with a hearing impairment, students who rely on visual patterning and students who have difficulty with auditory processing.

* The student looks at the word while the teacher reads the word aloud.
* The student studies the word by reading it, spelling it, and reading it again.
* The student closes eyes and attempts to spell the word orally two times without the model.
* Finally, the student attempts to write the word without the model.

Auditory Learners

227. If the student relies heavily on auditory skills to learn new words, the following steps may be implemented into the spelling program. This method may be appropriate for some students with visual impairments and students with fine motor difficulties.

   * The student observes the teacher reading, spelling and writing the word.
   * The student reads the word and repeats the letters verbally after the teacher.
   * Once again the student listens to the teacher spell the word; the student repeats it after the teacher.
   * The student spells the word without assistance.

Multisensory Approach

228. A cover and write method is appropriate for the student who prefers a multisensory approach.

   * The student looks at the word and pronounces it.
   * The student spells the word aloud.
   * The student covers the word and writes it down.
   * The student compares the word to the model.
   * If the student has written the word correctly, the student practices the word three times. (If the word is incorrect, the student repeats the entire process).
   * A final check is made. If all the words are correct, the student moves to the next word.

229. Allow the student to experiment with various programs. The student will be able to choose a study method that best meets their individual needs. If the student continues to do poorly on final assessments, encourage the student to try a different study method.

230. Periodically have the student practice with a peer, teacher or paraprofessional to ensure the student is practicing the words correctly. When practicing alone, frequently check to make sure the student is practicing correctly.

Spelling Tests

For some students, spelling tests produce a great deal of anxiety. Not only do they need to learn to spell the word, some students may also need to learn to read the words. For those who experience difficulty with fine motor, so much effort is placed into creating a legible product, that the actual spelling of the word escapes the student. Some students just cannot keep the same pace as others during a group test.

231. Test the student orally instead of in writing. Give the student an index card or paper with the score to turn in to the general education teacher.

232. Write the response for the student, especially for students with severe fine motor difficulty.

233. Cue the student as to the number of letters in each word when working with silent letters. This will help the phonetic speller remember the silent letters.

234. Test students over several words daily instead of one final test.

235. Allow the student to take the test with the special education teacher or paraprofessional at a separate time. Use the group test as practice test.

236. With the lower functioning student allow the student to select the correct spelling flashcard (word recognition goal).

237. If the student needs long periods of time to process information, give the student a prerecorded version of the test. The student is able to stop the tape and think about the word for as long as needed.

238. If the student reverses letters frequently, ask the student to spell the word orally. Allow credit for the correct oral response.

Grading

239. Record pretest and final test scores. Consider giving two grades. One based on the improvement between the pretest and final test score and a percentage score.

240. Encourage students to self-monitor their spelling progress by charting pretest and final test scores. Many students are motivated by self-monitoring techniques.

241. Have the student set a weekly spelling goal. Reward the student if the individual goal is met even if the student does not obtain the required class percentage.

242. Be sure to adhere to changes in grading or criteria noted on the Individualized Education Plan.

"Enlarge the opportunity and the person will expand to fill it!"

Eli Ginzberg

"In the end, we retain from our studies only that which we practically apply."
Johan Wolfgang Von Goethe

Chapter Seven

Mathematics

Many students receive special education service for math. Difficulties in mathematics manifest themselves in many ways. Number reversals are common. For many students complex word problems are difficult, as the student must be able to complete multiple steps, understand specific vocabulary, and often perform several types of calculations within the same word problem. Students are often required to memorize material such as addition and multiplication facts. Since math skills are built upon previously learned skills, students who lack the basic skills experience difficulty with advanced mathematics. Often students are required to copy math problems. For many, it is difficult to line up the columns or copy the numbers from a model, as the numbers are unrelated to one another. Auditory processing, visual processing, difficulty sequencing, and transferring information from the short into the long term memory are only a few of the factors which impact math.

When learning basic math skills, some students require the use of concrete manipulative material. When using manipulative material, the student first must demonstrate the operation using concrete materials. Often, when the answer is obtained, the student is required to hold the information in the short term memory and then transfer the answer to paper. Since many students with disabilities experience difficulty with memory, this is no simple task! For some students, the use of manipulative material causes confusion, as they do not see the relationship between the concrete material and the actual problem.

It is also important to analyze the curriculum used in the classroom. At the elementary level, some mathematic programs present new concepts daily, and allow minimal time for drill and practice activities. Although the concept continues to be recycled throughout the upcoming lessons, for the student with a disability often there is not enough drill and practice time to actually internalize the concept. When the concept is recycled through the program, the student may feel as though it is new, and has little recollection of learning the skill previously. For some students, the concepts may need to be regrouped allowing for daily drill and practice.

In the upper-grades, many students experience difficulty because they have not mastered the basic skills. For example the student who has not learned the basic skills of addition and subtraction certainly will have difficulty with multiplication and division. As the student advances through the grades, the prerequisite skills required increase and the student tends to fall further behind.

When providing service to the student with disabilities in the math setting, refer to the chapters entitled Daily Assignments and Testing Procedures. Both of these chapters have many practical ideas that can be adapted to the area of mathematics.

General Teaching Strategies

243. Many students with disabilities experience difficulty with abstract concepts. Introduce math concepts in "real life" situations. This relationship will help students understand the reason for the concept. Brainstorm and create a class list of ways math is used daily. When a new concept is taught, refer to the original list and decide why the skill is important. Add additional ideas. Here are some ideas that demonstrate daily use of math.

Percentages: calculate clothing discounts, interest on savings accounts or statistics from the local sports teams.

Graphs: Graph test scores, weather conditions for a month, or analyze individual eating habits by graphing the kinds of food consumed during a week.

Addition, subtraction, and decimals: maintain and balance a checking or savings account.

Measurement: double recipes for favorite foods or measure the classroom and create a new design on graph paper.

Time: public transportation schedules, television schedules, or calculate employment time cards.

244. When teaching new mathematical concepts, do not worry about perfect calculations. First teach the concept and be sure the student understands the process. The use of manipulative material and diagrams help many students.

245. Teach key math terms separately. Provide a dictionary of math terminology. Include simple drawings and examples to illustrate the terms and the various steps of the problems.

246. When teaching abstract concepts, use drawings, diagrams and visual demonstrations to help the student establish the relationship.

247. Use colored chalk or markers when demonstrating new skills. This will help direct the student's attention to the important points. For example color-code the groups of ones, tens, or hundreds when teaching regrouping of numbers.

248. Many commercial math practice pages include mixed problems on a page. A common example is a math practice page with both addition and subtraction problems. Ask the student to highlight and complete one operation first before proceeding to the next.

249. Cluster math problems into groups. Teach one skill at a time. If the assignment includes several types of math calculations on one page, provide ample drill and practice on one skill before moving on to the next skill.

250. Demonstrate and teach the relationship between math fact families. Look for patterns. This will help to establish the relationship between numbers.

251. If applicable, model math problems using manipulative material. When modeling, explain each step verbally to the student. During student practice sessions, ask the student to also verbalize each step. Listen to the student. You will be able to understand the student's thought process and easily analyze why the student is experiencing difficulty.

252. When teaching strategies for numberline use, create a long numberline on the floor for the student to walk on. This will also assist the student with directionality.

253. Demonstrate how to use the numberline for addition, subtraction, and counting by groups. For students who reverse numbers it can be used as a close up reference tool. For the older student, who may be embarrassed to use one, demonstrate how a face clock (watch) a ruler can serve the same purpose and is not quite as obvious.

254. When teaching the concept of money, use real money in place of paper or cardboard money. For a student with visual processing, it is very difficult to tell the difference between coins on worksheets.

Provide actual practice time by setting up a store. Provide paper money for students to buy school supplies such as paper, pencils, rulers or whatever is needed for the school day. When materials are returned, the student is refunded the money. The prices can be changed daily.

Another option is to provide old catalogs and grocery store ads. Ask the student to create a shopping list and purchase the items.

255. Provide ample workspace on worksheets so students do not need to transfer information.

256. Use computer programs in place of timed tests. The quantity and practice time can be preset on many commercial math programs. For some students you may want to double the computer time and divide the results by two. This will provide a fairly accurate result. It also allows the student a little additional time to get organized and adjust to the computer.

257. Ask students to graph the information from timed tests. Look for improvement. For the majority of students with disabilities, timed tests cause a great amount frustration.

258. Frequently review and reinforce previously taught skills. Start each math class with a daily review of the concept taught the previous day. As a teacher you will be able to see check whether or not the students retained the information from the previous lesson. If not, review or reteach the lesson. In math this is especially important as many of the new skills are built upon previously learned skills.

259. Many students with disabilities need immediate feedback on their assignments. Math centers are an excellent way to review and reinforce previously taught concepts. The following math centers can be set up with minimal effort. Multiple level activities may be included in the centers so students of all ability levels can easily participate. Self - correction sheets may be included or students may be assigned to cooperative groups. Here are some suggestions to get you started.

The Restaurant – Ask students to collect take-out menus from various local establishments. The student selects a menu, chooses several individual items, and then determines the total cost of the items, including the tax and tip. If you would like the student to self-check, create a selection of individual restaurant cards. On the front of the card write the name of the restaurant and specific menu items. On the back of the card write the steps to complete the process and the answer. Laminate the cards.

The Store – In this center, create a grocery store, toy store or clothing store. Provide a collection of various catalogs, newspaper, and grocery store ads. For older students you may want to include special sales and provide check blanks and a check register to record purchases. A store credit card could also be available, allowing the student to calculate the monthly payment with interest. Once again the student may purchase items, or specific directions with self-check cards may be provided.

Furnish A Home Center – In this center a collection of catalogs with home furnishings are needed. The student can create their dream room or furnish a home with an allotted budget. Older students can actually measure their room and purchase only items that would actually fit. With catalog specifications for the lengths and widths of the furniture, students can use graph paper and create the actual layout.

The Manipulative Center – In this center you may want to include geoboards, tangrams, and pattern blocks.

The Computer Center – In this center include math programs for student review and programs related to current math objectives. You may want to include a signup sheet and a clock or timer, so all students have an opportunity to participate.

260. When teaching word problems, simplify the vocabulary and take out the irrelevant information. Teach the key words that are associated with word problems. When teaching word problems it is helpful to do the following:

First, ask the student to read the problem to determine the question.

Reread the problem. Look for key words. Some of the key words are: altogether, together, in all, are left, spent or remain.

If applicable draw a diagram of the word problem.

Write out the problem. Estimate the answer before solving it. If the estimated answer seems reasonable, solve the problem.

261. Develop task analysis sheets for the basic areas of mathematics. Use these checklists to determine the specific areas of difficulty. Look for error patterns in daily assignments. If a student has extreme difficulty with a problem or process, ask the student to verbalize the steps. Some students experience difficulties because a step has been eliminated or they are performing a step incorrectly. Patterns of errors usually emerge in the following areas: inadequate knowledge of facts, incorrect operations, or the use of ineffective strategies.

Parallel Math Activities

Some students are unable and will never be able to complete the same curriculum as the rest of the class. For these students it is important to be aware of the goals and objectives on the Individualized Educational Plan. When support is available, often the supplementary materials can correspond with the current class activity. Listed below are just a few ideas for activities that can be completed with a paraprofessional or peer tutor.

262. Decide whether or not the skill is a "functional" life skill. Functional skills are the skills that will support the student in independent living.

In the classroom keep an assortment of materials the student can do independently. These materials may be stored in a basket. Be sure the student knows where the special basket is located. The basket may include dice (basic facts), calculator with self-correctors, flashcards, clock activities, puzzles and classifying activities. All of the activities should be activities the student can work on independently – until support arrives.

263. Provide supplemental materials in the same content area as the rest of the class. For example, if the class is learning addition with regrouping, the student may work on basic addition facts. It is possible the student can still be involved in the discussion, demonstration and use same manipulative material, if the general education teacher varies the questions and directs specific questions toward the student.

264. Correlate the objectives from the Individualized Education Plan with the instruction. If the student's goal is number recognition, use the daily assignment or the classroom textbook to practice. If the objective is to be able to correctly write the numbers, the student could copy problems from the general education textbook.

265. Order a supplemental text for the student's direct instruction. Direct instruction can be provided for the student when the class is receiving instruction. During independent work time, the student will be able to complete the assignment in the supplementary text.

266. Purchase inexpensive dot-to-dot books at local stores. The dot-to-dot activities help with number sequencing and recognition.

267. Work on number formation with the use of tracers or templates.

268. Make a set of number cards. Use the cards to work on the chronological sequencing of numbers. Use the same cards for one-to-one correspondence, ordering from least to greatest and number recognition.

269. Provide the student with mathematical symbol cards. The student can use the cards to make mathematical equations. The student may copy the equation onto paper.

270. Collect shells, beads, seeds, various shaped pasta and buttons. Put them into boxes or bags. Use these collections to sort and classify objects. The materials may also be used to assist with one-to-one correspondence.

271. Use egg cartons to sort various materials and establish the concept of *group*. Use this concept of group to introduce addition and subtraction.

272. Teach the student to use a calculator. Allow the student to do some of the textbook problems with a calculator.

273. Have the student collate papers in chronological order.

274. Coordinate the student's assessments, daily assignments, and rewards with the general math class.

275. Create games the student may play with other students in the classroom. Activities can easily be included into math centers explained in idea #259. Vary the peer group.

Adapting Math Assignments

276. Place colored arrows on the student's worksheet to assist with directionality. Often students try to perform math calculations from left to right (as with reading), instead of right to left.

277. Draw lines between the columns of math problems so the student is able to record the information in the correct column.

278. Box in or highlight the ones column so the student knows where to begin the math calculation.

279. To help students line up columns, turn lined notebook paper so the lines run vertically instead of horizontally, or use graph paper for instant organization.

280. Purchase consumable texts from the publisher. Students with fine motor difficulty will not have to copy problems and will be able to spend more time with the actual calculations.

281. If consumable texts are unavailable, enlarge the text so the student may write on the photocopied page.

282. When working with problem solving activities, emphasize the problem solving steps, not the final answer. Many students do not participate for fear their final computation is incorrect.

283. Number the steps in word problems. Highlight the important words.

284. Allow the student to use charts, tables, and calculators when the process of addition, subtraction, multiplication and division is understood.

285. When using addition or multiplication charts, provide the student with a cutout "L". This will assist the student to find the intersection box of columns and rows.

286. Use good judgement. Some students are able to memorize basic facts, so allow ample amount of time before providing a calculator. For others, memorization may be extremely difficult and you may want to use a calculator from the beginning.

Student Aids

287. When teaching multiple step calculations, write the steps of the process for students to use as a guide. Provide a visual model next to the written steps so the student can see the correlation between the model and the written problem.

   Division is an example of a process that requires multiple steps. The mnemonic "dad, mother, sister, brother" which stands for divide, multiply, subtract, bring-down is often used.

288. Create a small booklet for the student to keep as a math reference book. The booklet should include the basic math concepts covered in the class. The student can then refer to the guide if confused about a mathematical operation. Include the math vocabulary and a visual diagram for each step.

289. Attach a numberline to the student's desk or in the math book. This will assist the student with addition, subtraction and the correct formation of the numbers. This will also assist students who experience difficulties with number reversals.

290. Teach the student to use the face clock in the classroom as a number line for facts to 12. This will support the student who is opposed to having a numberline placed on the desk.

291. Create a chart with two numberlines. Label one for addition with an arrow to the right and label the other chart for subtraction with an arrow running to the left. This will help the student internalize the concept.

292. Allow the student to use rubber number stamps or a computer if number formation is extremely difficult.

293. Allow the student to use a calculator for all math calculations once the process and the concept are mastered.

294. Use stick-on notes to help the student keep his/her place in the text.

295. *Touch Math* is an excellent program for students who struggle with computation. Touchpoints or black dots are placed strategically on numbers 1-9 and the students touch the points and count either forward for addition or backwards for subtraction. *Touch Math* can be used in addition, subtraction, multiplication and division. This program is available from Innovative Learning Concepts, Inc., in Denver, CO.

"One person's constant is another person's variable."

Susan Gerhart

"Expect the best, plan for the worst and prepare to be surprised."

Denis Waitley

Chapter Eight

Organizational Skills

"I can't find my homework. I know I turned it in! I know I did it!" Does this sound familiar?

Students with disabilities can complete assignments when adapted to their specific needs, but frequently the assignment is lost or misplaced. Some students experience difficulty with organization of time and others of their physical space. Some appear to be unorganized because they are unable to follow oral and written directions.

This section focuses on organization of the physical environment of the student.

Classroom Organization

As an educator, consider your personal organizational skills. Think about how you personally organize your time and space. Now step back and look at the classroom environment. Is the classroom organized? Is there a specific location for supplies, materials and books? Is there a designated location to turn in assignments? Is the seating arrangement conducive for learning? Is there a space for paraprofessionals and volunteers to organize and keep their supplies? The adult must evaluate the current environment.

It is hard to expect the student to be organized if the necessary tools are not in place and the expectations are not consistent.

296. Provide the student with a simplified map of the school. Number and highlight classroom locations. Include the most direct route for the student.

297. Write the daily schedule on the board and try to follow it as closely as possible. Some students need to anticipate what will occur next in the school day. Also check to be sure the student is able to tell time. Many homes have only digital clocks. If the classroom has a face clock, be sure the student knows how to read it.

298. Organize the classroom. Provide a specific location to hand in daily assignments, late assignments, and a place to pick up take-home materials.

299. Develop a classroom routine and follow it. If possible, take breaks at approximately the same time each day. Allow the student several extra minutes to organize materials.

300. Color code folders for each subject. If possible coordinate folders with the colors of the textbook.

301. Keep all student supplies in a central area. Clearly state which materials the student may use during the day. If there are specific materials that should not used by students, put them away.

302. Create seating arrangements that allow the student to see the board easily without turning their body.

Student Organization

303. Use color coded folders for academic areas. Keep a pencil, pen, paper, and other necessary items in each folder.

304. If folders are confusing for the student, use a three-ring notebook. Keep all folders and paper in one notebook. Instruct the student to keep assignments in the notebook, until it is time to hand it in. Use a three-hole punch for loose papers and insert into the notebook. This is great for the student who has extreme difficulty with organization.

305. Ask students to clean and organize the desk or locker at least once a week. Organize papers into three piles: file into folders, take home and toss. Sharpen pencils and throw away old pencils and pens.

306. Provide the student with subject headings for all papers. This will help students to put papers into the appropriate folder.

307. Develop a color code chart and post it, or have the student keep a crayon that matches the corresponding folder and color code the corner of each assignment. With written assignments, it is easy to confuse a social studies rough draft report with an English rough draft report, especially at the secondary level.

308. Often students need to be taught how to organize. Allow students time to discuss and share their individual organizational strategies. List the ideas and encourage the students to experiment with various methods of organization.

309. Use a homework book or an assignment sheet. Explain the difference between the words "due" and "do". Teach the student to prioritize assignments by estimating the amount of time the assignment will take in relation to the due date.

Some students need a daily, weekly and monthly calendar to understand the concept of time.

310. When assigning projects, list the approximate length of time needed to complete the assignment. With complex assignments, provide specific dates for the various steps. Check the assignments on the specified due dates to make sure the student is keeping pace.

311. Supply the student with a pad of "Assignments to Do Today". Help the student to write reminder notes.

312. Use a peer to help monitor assignments. The peer can assist the student in placing assignments in correct folders or turning in assignments.

313. For students who have difficulty remembering to do homework, permit the student to call home and leave a message on a recorder. Make sure the student notes the subject and page number of assignments. Teenagers may forget the homework assignment, but they always seem to check the telephone for messages! In this day of modern technology, some students have resorted to leaving messages on their pagers or sending an e-mail to their home computer.

314. Allow the student to check out an extra set of textbooks for home use.

315. Provide the student a packet of Post-It™ notes. The student can write down each assignment as given. The note can be placed on the student's desk. The student may throw the note when the assignment is complete or stick it into their assignment book.

316. Create a simple daily checklist with assignments and reminders. The student can tape it onto the top of the desk or into a notebook. When the assignment is complete, the student crosses it off the list. If daily assignments remain,

the student can staple or tape the checklist into their assignment book.

317. If an assignment is completed during the class period, encourage the student to turn it in immediately instead of waiting until the next day.

318. Plastic zip lock bags can be used to store pencils, crayons, markers and supplies in the student's desk. Students who have difficulty with organization may want to keep several individual bags in their desks or lockers. Periodically reorganize and restock the bags.

319. Provide extra time for students with organizational difficulties to locate materials and organize materials before beginning a new lesson. Let students know a transition is about to occur, by using a visual or auditory signal. Turn the lights off/on, ring a bell, play some music, or clap your hands. Once the signal is given, allow students 2-3 additional minutes to put away supplies and prepare for the next activity.

320. When monitoring students on a daily basis (check-in and check-out), go into the student's classroom. The student will not miss valuable class time or important directions. Use this time to check assignment books and assignments listed on the board.

321. Teach the student to monitor their private self-talk. Often disorganized students feel frustrated and begin to think negative thoughts such as "I can't do this. I just don't understand. I'll never get it!" Have the student practice taking several deep breaths and repeat positive statements such as "I can do this. I will be able to understand it. Slow down and focus." When directions become complex, ask the student to verbalize the steps.

322. Enlist parent cooperation with setting a specific time daily time for homework. Send a supply list home so parents

know what is needed. Be specific. Not all homes have calculators, protractors, and rulers on hand.

If the student does not have homework, time should be spent reading, or cleaning and organizing their folders and backpack.

323. Assign a hanging folder, a numbered file folder or mailbox to each student. Daily assignments may be placed immediately into the folder for safekeeping.

"To get what you want, STOP doing what isn't working."

Dennis Weaver

"The man who makes hard things easy is the educator."

Thomas Edison

Chapter Nine

Directions

Each day a student is bombarded with hundreds of directions. Many students with disabilities experience difficulty in school because they are not able to process directions. Inattention, difficulty with auditory processing, memory deficits, poor listening skills, limited receptive language or the inability to sequence information are only a few of the reasons. No matter what the root of the problem is, it is often a very frustrating experience for the student.

Oral Directions

324. Be sure you nave the student's attention before giving directions. Pause and wait if you do not. Eye contact is important.

325. Change the format of oral directions. Provide directions in written format so the student can refer to the information frequently.

326. Do not give irrelevant information during oral directions. Keep directions concise and simple.

327. Simplify the vocabulary.

328. When giving verbal explanations if possible, use visuals also.

329. Divide lengthy and complex directions into one or two step segments. When directions are complex, allow students to complete the first step before adding additional directions.

330. Appoint a peer tutor to coach the student through multiple step directions.

331. Monitor the student's understanding by asking the student to repeat the direction to you or a peer.

332. Use a combination of visual and auditory directions for the student. Use the blackboard, the overhead or a flip chart.

333. Include rebus pictures with written directions for students who are unable to read the directions.

334. Photograph the steps of experiments, demonstrations and activities that have multiple steps. Glue photographs in chronological order inside a file folder. The student may use this folder if a visual aid is needed. File directions with the unit for future use.

335. Record daily assignments on tape. The student may listen to the directions as many times as needed. Include the due dates. Encourage the student to write down incomplete assignments into a homework notebook.

336. If the student has a hearing impairment, appoint a peer to cue the student when oral directions are given. Be sure the student is also cued into intercom messages. Always check for understanding.

Written Directions

337. Write the directions in sequential order. If there are multiple steps, number the steps.

338. Allow sufficient time for the student to copy the assignment. If the student is unable to copy from a distant model, allow him/her to copy from a peer or appoint a peer to write the directions for the student.

339. Accompany written directions with a visual demonstration or model whenever possible.

340. Ask the student to read the written directions at least two times. Allow the student extra time to underline or highlight key words and phrases.

341. When there is a string of directions at the beginning of the assignment, have the student place a colored dot between each segment of the instruction.

342. Always check for understanding before the student begins the assignment.

343. For visually impaired students always give test directions, assignments and important directions orally.

344. Place a piece of yellow acetate over the page of print to enhance the contrast and darken the print for the visually impaired.

345. Use black flair pens to trace over directions and darken the print for students with low vision.

346. For visually impaired students, use a white board with erasable black marker, or if available, a green chalkboard in place of a blackboard.

MRS. KING SPORTS HER
WORN SOFTBALL CAP AS A REMINDER
THAT INDIVIDUALIZING TO MEET
UNIQUE STUDENT NEEDS IS
OLD HAT TO GOOD TEACHERS.

Source: "Flying by the Seat of Your Pants: More Absurdities and Realities of Special Education" by Michael F. Giangreco © 1999 Reprinted with permission.

"Children are apt to live up to what you believe of them."

Lady Bird Johnson

Chapter Ten

Large Group Instruction

Oral Presentations

For students, a large portion of the day is spent listening to the general or special education teacher present material orally. At the secondary level, the majority of the day is spent in lecture sessions. This can be a frustrating experience for the student who experiences difficulty with auditory processing, taking notes or sustaining attention for large periods of time.

Periodically videotape a class presentation to analyze your personal presentation style and student participation. You may want to explain to the students the reason for a self-evaluation. It is important for students to realize that even as adults we are continually striving for improvement. When viewing the presentation think about the following questions. Is the rate in which you speak too fast, too slow, or is it appropriate for the lesson? Is your vocabulary at an appropriate level for the target group of students? Do students seem actively engaged in the learning process? Do you frequently check for understanding? Is the lesson sequential, or do you randomly jump from topic to topic? When viewing, take notes on the areas you feel are exceptionally good and note the areas that you would like to improve.

The following section provides ideas for educators and for students.

347. Always state the goals and objectives of the lesson at the beginning of the session. Write the goals and objectives on the blackboard for reference.

348. Begin the day with a review of the previous lesson, important points presented, and vocabulary so the student is able to build on prior information.

349. Provide all information in a logically organized and sequential format.

350. Present only relevant information during lectures. Use nouns in place of pronouns whenever possible. The consistent use of pronouns may cause confusion to some students, especially if they did not understand or pay attention at the beginning or if the lecturer moves rapidly from one topic to another.

351. Simplify the vocabulary, especially when the student is required to take notes. Highlight important information on overhead transparencies.

352. When giving oral presentations, provide visual aids for the student. Emphasize important subject material by using colored chalk on the blackboard and colored markers on overheads and charts. Highlight key words, phrases, and steps to math problems.

353. Pause frequently when giving an oral presentation. Ask the student to summarize information. Ask specific questions to check for understanding. Relate new information to previously learned concepts as much as possible.

354. Be sure the student removes all unnecessary materials from the desktop during lectures and oral presentations. During oral presentations, the student should have two sharpened pencils, paper and a highlighter on top of the desk.

355. Vary the level of questioning during the classroom discussions so all students can participate.

Make special arrangements for those students who are perceived by others as "never having the correct answer". Provide the student with specific questions and ask the student to look for the answers before the actual presentation. Let the student know in advance which questions he/she will be called on to answer.

Encourage active participation by using whole group response. There are several ways to incorporate whole group response.

* Provide each student with a small chalkboard, an old sock and a piece of chalk. Students work alone or in partners to formulate a short answer response. Allow ample time for the student to write their responses.

* Index cards can be used to respond to true/false or agree/disagree statements. Once the question is asked the students show their response by holding up their card.

* Thumbs up/thumbs down is another simple way to encourage active group participation during presentations. Once again, be sure to allow ample time for the student to process the question before asking for the response.

Note Taking Skills

Note taking is a difficult process. Think about the last time you attended a class or a workshop and were required to take notes. Did you write on the syllabus provided? Perhaps you brought a tape player and recorded the information so you could listen to it in your car or during a quiet time at home. Did you jot down key words and phrases? Or did you write entire phrases verbatim? Perhaps you were able to generalize the information and fill in a chart or a graph. When the presenter stated, "This is important!" Did you furiously try to write every word?

Taking notes is not a simple skill. It requires the student to process information both auditory and visually and then output the information in written format. Students must be taught various strategies to take notes successfully.

356. Encourage the student to write notes using their own words.

357. Encourage students to use abbreviations during note taking. You may want to post a list of common abbreviations.

358. Provide the student with an outline of the main topics. Provide ample space so the student is able to take notes directly on the outline.

359. List major points on the blackboard or overhead before or during the presentation. When the presentation is complete, use the following technique to immediately reinforce the key concepts of the lesson.

Ask students to fold a piece of notebook paper in half to create two columns. In the left column ask the students to list the major points from the blackboard. Leave three blank lines between each major point. When the presentation is finished ask the student to recall and write as much as they can remember about each specific point. When finished allow time for the students to compare their responses and add additional information. This may also be used as a study guide.

360. Before lecturing, provide a list of discussion questions to the student. This will help students focus on the general idea instead of many small details.

361. Cue the student to the major points with the use of key phrases, such as *please remember this*, *this point is very important*, or *write this down*, during the presentation.

362. When comparing and contrasting information, provide a chart or a Venn diagram for the student to complete.

363. When presenting information in chronological order, provide the student with a timeline. Include the starting and ending points. For some students, additional reference points need to be included.

364. Encourage students to jot down key words if there is not enough time to complete the entire thought.

365. If providing a visual demonstration, allow the student sufficient time to copy the material into the notes. At the end of the class period, allow a few additional minutes for students to compare their information to the visual aid. For complex material, provide photocopies of the transparencies to the students.

366. If the student is unable to take notes, allow a peer to use carbon paper to create a copy, or make a photocopy. The student should still take notes during the presentation and actively participate in the lesson.

367. Allow time at the end of oral presentations for students to compare and discuss their notes in small group settings. This will help students to reinforce the concepts learned and to clarify the points that were not fully understood.

368. At the end of each presentation take a few minutes to summarize the lesson. Place closure on the lesson by asking students to list or verbalize the main points of the lecture. Ask the students to look for and highlight this important information in their notes.

369. When using an overhead, allow the student with low vision to look directly into the overhead projector while the transparency is projected onto the wall.

370. An overhead projector also helps students with hearing impairments. It allows the student to see the presentation and read the teacher's lips simultaneously.

371. When presenting material orally, simultaneously record the presentation. This will assist students who may need additional reinforcement of the current lesson. It also benefits the student who is absent.

"Ability is what you're capable of doing. Motivation determines what you do. Attitude determines how well you will do it."

Lou Holtz

"When grades become the substitute for learning, and when they become more important than what is learned, they tend to lower academic achievement."

William Glasser

Chapter Eleven

Classroom Assessments

For many students the word *test* produces large amounts of anxiety. In a society where testing is often the major form of evaluation, it is important that students understand how the assessment actually affects their overall grade. If the test weighs relatively light in relation to projects, daily assignments and class participation, make sure students are aware of this. To help relieve test anxiety, provide sample practice tests and assessments for students. Simple strategies such as showing students how to eliminate answers on multiple choice tests and finding key words on essay tests will help students become better test takers. If appropriate, allow students an opportunity to retake tests.

Some students require alternate forms of assessment due to difficulties with reading and written language. When developing alternate forms of assessment, there are two areas to keep in mind. First, be sure the accommodations used on daily assignments are incorporated into the assessment. For example, if the textbook is read aloud or taped for the student, this same accommodation should be used in a testing situation. Secondly, keep the objective of the assessment in mind. If the goal is to measure the student's knowledge of the curriculum, it is important to assess only the curriculum and not penalize the student by focusing on the student's limitations.

Many students with special needs have difficulty with short and long term memory. Often assessments become memory tests as the student is asked to recall facts, figures and specific data presented during class presentations. When developing or using specific tests, read the test and determine whether the test measures the student's ability to memorize specific data or whether it measures the true learning of information.

When assessing students, consider using authentic assessments, demonstrations and portfolios as alternatives to the traditional paper / pencil assessments.

372. Allow the student to test orally with a peer, the general or special education teacher, or the paraprofessional.

373. Permit the student to demonstrate the concept or illustrate what was learned.

374. Write the answers to the questions for the student. Be sure to record the answers verbatim.

375. Allow extra time to complete the test. If extra time cannot be provided, consider grading the student only on the items completed.

376. Read all test directions orally. Ask students to repeat the test directions to either a teacher or peer. Frequently students do not follow or perhaps misunderstand the instructions which results in a poor test score.

377. When administering final grades, make sure you are aware of the mastery criteria on the Individualized Educational Plan.

378. Tape record the test and allow students to tape record their answers.

379. If the test permits, allow students to respond only to the even or odd numbered problems.

380. Maintain a record of the pretests and posttests. Give a final grade on individual progress and improvement. A student who fails a pretest and receives a 50% on a posttest has made great strides in comparison to the student who has an 80% on a pretest and 90% on a posttest.

381. Limit the number of concepts presented on each test.

382. Divide the test into segments. Each segment should have an individual set of directions. Grade each segment of the test individually. This will help determine the areas to reteach.

383. Test frequently to monitor progress. Give short daily quizzes. The student's progress can easily be monitored and a determination can be made whether additional teaching or reinforcement is needed.

384. Circle, underline, or have the student highlight key words within the directions.

385. The student may need to test individually with the special education teacher or paraprofessional.

386. Use recognition of facts rather than factual recall on tests. Delete the trick questions on commercially made tests.

387. If the district requires the student to take standardized tests, order consumable tests. This eliminates the need for the student to transfer their response to a computer score sheet. Errors often occur when transferring information.

388. Most standardized tests rely heavily on the student's ability to read the material. If the student's reading level is several years below grade level, this will be a frustrating experience. Address this issue during the IEP meeting. If the student does not participate in standardized testing, it must be addressed in the Individual Education Plan.

389. If students are required by law to take standardized tests, compare the test results to the individualized testing records in the special education folder. If the results on standardized testing are severely discrepant, you may want place a note on the standardized test indicating that individual ability and achievement scores are listed in the Individual Education Plan.

AUTHENTIC ASSESSMENT:
CONSIDER THE ALTERNATIVES.

Source: "Flying by the Seat of Your Pants: More Absurdities and Realities of Special Education"
by Michael F. Giangreco © 1999 Reprinted with permission.

This page may not be reproduced

Teacher Made Tests

Formal and informal assessments occur daily in the classroom setting. When creating teacher made or curriculum based assessments, use the following guidelines.

390. Write directions in a clear, precise format.

391. Include one direction per sentence.

392. Underline or box the directions. This will help to separate the information from the remainder of the text.

393. Provide examples of correct responses. This will act as a visual aid for the student.

394. Use large bold print whenever possible.

395. Leave ample space between problems. Avoid making tests that have a cluttered appearance.

396. Avoid using words such as never, not, sometimes and always.

397. When creating multiple-choice tests, exclude statements such as *all of the above* or *none of the above.*

398. When creating matching tests, organize both columns so the students' choices are clear and concise. Present the matching statements and answers in blocks of five. Double space between the blocks of information.

399. When creating true and false tests, eliminate words such as *all* or *never.* Avoid using double negatives. They are easily misinterpreted.

400. Create fill in the blank tests by placing the choices under the blank space instead of at the end of the sentence.

401. When giving essay tests, provide the student with a blank outline format, so the student may organize ideas before beginning to write. Highlight or underline key words in the essay questions.

402. Provide individual portfolios for students to collect and save their work. The students should place their best work in the portfolio. All portfolio selections should be in the final format. Students, teachers and parents can easily note the progress the student has made over a period of time. This may be used as an alternate form of assessment.

403. Allow the student to demonstrate the knowledge learned by performing or demonstrating key concepts. Following are several examples to assess Math or Science skills.

   Math
   In place of paper and pencil tests, provide the student with authentic situations. Provide younger students grocery store advertisements and ask the students to purchase items and list the price for the total purchases.

   Collect old catalogs. Provide the student with a specific amount of money to purchase gifts for a family of six, furnish a room or buy school supplies.

   Older students may balance a check book, calculate bank interest rates, and percentage of taxes taken from paychecks. Batting averages, clothing store discounts and sales tax are of interest to older students. Depending upon the skill assessed, the directions may be simple or complex.

   Science
   The following are types of performance assessments for environmental units. For example, during a weather unit the student can document temperatures, explain high and low pressure areas from the newspaper weather maps and document types of clouds present.

Students can collect samples of simple and compound leaves. The leaves can then be labeled and categorized into groups.

Students may collect different types of insects and label body parts. The insects may be categorized into groups.

Science experiments can be completed in cooperative groups and the results of the experiment explained to the class.

404. Allow the student to create an audio or videocassette demonstrating knowledge of the content area. This is especially good for those students who have difficulty speaking or sharing in front of the entire group.

Alternate Grading Systems

Several grading alternatives may be considered for students with special needs. Many educators use a traditional percentage grading system. This system may not be appropriate for all students.

405. The student's IEP will provide the framework for grading. Be sure you are aware of the criteria.

406. If the test includes various sections testing multiple areas, grade each section individually. For example, if the test includes a true/false section, multiple-choice and essay section, provide an individual grade for each section. This helps determine the preferred testing style of the student. The student will also be able to determine the area which needs more practice or additional reinforcement. If a student continually fails a specific type of assessment, such as the multiple-choice section, the student can be taught strategies to improve the performance of that specific area.

When testing various skills, for example in math, you will be able to determine the specific skill area which the student experiences difficulty.

407. Contract grading is often used in inclusive settings. The student and teacher determine the quantity and quality of work the student must complete to receive a specific grade in a subject area.

408. Combination grading can reward students for their performance and help individualize the grading process. In combination grading, the student's grade is based on their ability, effort and achievement. The ability grade is based on the expected amount of improvement in the subject area. The effort grade is based on the amount of time and effort the student puts into the assignment to master the concept. The achievement grade is related to the student's mastery in relation to others in the class. These three individual grades can be averaged together for the final grade.

409. Shared grading is frequently used in inclusive settings. With shared grading, the regular and the special education teacher collaborate to assign the grade. The final grade is based on the grades and observations of both teachers.

410. A pass/fail system may be appropriate for some students. This system acknowledges that the student has completed the required assignments as determined by the teachers and the IEP.

411. If the report card does not correspond to the student's individual goals and objectives on the IEP, write descriptive comments. List the skills that have been mastered. This is an appropriate time to review the IEP and discuss the goals and objectives for the student.

"The real contest is always between what you've done and what you're capable of doing. You measure yourself against yourself and nobody else."

Geoffrey Gaberino

CONSIDERING HER STUDENTS WITHOUT
DISABILITIES, MRS. BAKER
REALIZES DAVID'S UNUSUAL
BEHAVIORS AREN'T THAT UNUSUAL.

Source: "Flying by the Seat of Your Pants: More Absurdities and Realities of Special Education"
by Michael F. Giangreco © 1999 Reprinted with permission.

"The A,B,C's of Inclusion: Acceptance, Belonging and Community"

Mary Beth Doyle

Chapter Twelve

Attention Difficulties

"I just don't know what to do anymore! The student is always out of his seat or walking around the room!" "The student is so disruptive in the classroom - it is affecting the other students." "The student seems to be in a dreamland. Even though she is looking at me, she doesn't seem to be able to focus on what I am saying or follow through on the assignments."

These are common concerns heard regularly by professionals and parents. Many students with special needs have difficulty sustaining attention. For some, it is an issue of maturity, for others the classroom structure may not be conducive to their individual learning style. For some of these students, changing the environment by providing more or perhaps less structure is beneficial. Perhaps some students in your classroom are medically diagnosed as ADD or ADHD. As indicated by the name, these students have difficulty sustaining attention. Attention is an important prerequisite for all learning and success in the school environment.

For all of the above students, accommodations need to be made within the classroom setting if the student is to experience success in school. If a student is diagnosed as ADD and is on medication, it is important to obtain a release of information from the parent and speak directly with the doctor or psychologist. Also, meet with the parents. Both the parents and doctor will be able to provide valuable information about the student. If possible adapt the strategies used in the home to the classroom setting. For the majority of the students, the accommodations discussed in this book will assist the student in achieving success in the classroom.

The strategies in this section pertain directly to the student who experiences difficulty with attention, on task behavior, impulsiveness or is easily distracted.

Structuring the Environment

Daily structure needs to be provided for all students, but for these students it is especially important. Transition times are difficult and should be closely monitored.

412. Keep a daily schedule on the board. Discuss the schedule and point out in advance any changes that will occur. Use signals such as turning the light off/on, ringing a bell or playing music as a gentle reminder the activity is coming to a close.

413. Provide extra structure during transition times. Allow the student a few additional minutes to adjust and organize materials before beginning a new subject.

414. Review the classroom rules frequently. If a student is having difficulty with a specific rule, write down the rule for the student. Be clear and concise. Provide the student with specific examples of the rule.

    Some students need to move. Make a simple red and green flip card. When the red side is showing it means the student needs to remain seated. When the green side is showing the student may quietly move about the room.

415. Always state what the student should do, instead of what the student should not do. If the student is running in the hall, simply say, "Walk, please."

416. Try to schedule the strong academic subjects in the morning.

417. Check-in and check-out times are important for the student. Enlist the support of the special education teacher or paraprofessional if the student has special needs. If not, obtain the support of the school social worker or counselor.

418. Encourage the student to keep a homework notebook. If a telephone is available, allow the student to call and leave a reminder for him/herself. For younger students a laminated "No Homework" card can be inserted into the homework notebook to communicate with the parent that all work is complete. Whatever system is used, be sure to hold the student responsible for all assignments.

419. A three-ring notebook with pocket folders will help keep all supplies, materials and assignments in one place. Instruct the student not to remove an assignment unless it is time to turn it in.

420. Allow the student to check out an extra copy of all of the textbooks for home use.

Behavior and Attention Difficulties

Reasons for inappropriate behaviors are many. It is best not to jump to the conclusion that the student is intentionally rude or disruptive. The student may simply not know or understand what they are to do at the given moment. The student may be entering a developmental stage different than his/her peers. For some students, oftentimes, ignoring the behavior will simply eliminate it.

When dealing with difficult students a person needs to think and respond, rather than react. When working with the student, it is important to remain calm and avoid debating or arguing with the student. As strong emotions increase, thinking skills and listening comprehension decreases. The student will read more from your body language, tone, cadence and the volume of your words than from the actual words. Keep your words short and simple. Make sure your body language and voice are giving the same message!

Help students to realize they do have choices. Providing specific examples and role-playing situations helps some students realize the type of choices they have. Keep a list of consequences for misbehavior and always administer the consequences consistently and immediately. Praise the student immediately for good behavior and try to "catch" the student in positive situations.

421. Make sure you have the student's attention when talking to him or her. Eye contact is important. Use private visual cues. Touching your eye means "look at me", your ear "time to listen", and the side of your mouth "no talking".

422. Provide small group instruction as much as possible. A small group provides more opportunity for participation thus increasing the student's chance to participate and stay on task.

423. Provide only one and two step directions. Check for understanding of each direction. Ask the student to repeat what he/she has just heard.

424. Give one assignment at a time. Be sure the student writes it down. Keep a daily list of assignments with due dates on the board. Ask students to copy the assignments into their assignment book.

425. Allow ample time for hands-on instruction. This will help actively engage the student in the learning process. Active participation is extremely important for this student. It will assist the student in remaining focused.

426. Modify daily assignments to alleviate frustration. (See the section on Daily Assignments).

427. Use computer programs for academic reinforcement if appropriate. This allows the student to receive immediate feedback. It also allows the student to self-pace the instruction and may help to increase motivation.

428. Use a timer to help the student stay focused. Set the timer to coincide with the amount of time you perceive the student is able to remain focused. Tell the student what you expect to be completed during the allotted time. When the student has adjusted to using a timer, play "Beat the Clock!" Challenge the student to complete the assignment before the timer rings. Gradually increase the time.

429. Allow time during the day for the student to get up, walk around and stretch. Provide a list of appropriate times.

430. Use random strategies when calling on students during large and small group activities. Place the students' names in a basket and randomly draw a name or use a deck of index cards and randomly select one. Since the students do not know who will be called on next, attention increases.

431. Provide forms of immediate feedback for the student. Self-correctors are appropriate for daily assignments. Many students benefit from the immediate feedback.

Impulsivity and Distractibility

"She just doesn't think!" "He always blurts out the answer before he is called on!" "She is always daydreaming." Some students tend to act without thinking and are easily distracted.

432. Place creative artwork in the back of the classroom to eliminate visual distractions for the student. Avoid cluttering walls with excessive amount of materials that may distract the student.

433. Check seating arrangements. Students who are easily distracted should not be seated near doors, windows or high traffic areas.

434. For the easily distracted student allow extra time to complete assignments, even when assignments have been modified. For some students, earplugs help block out background noise. For others, listening to soft music with earphones will block out some of the distracting stimuli.

435. Avoid timed activities and tests. Some students become frustrated when they notice others finished an assignment, which they have barely started. The student often will often guess or simply quit working. When giving group assessments, ask all students to remain in their seats and read quietly until everyone has finished. Collect the tests at the end of the session.

436. Ask the student to stop and think before responding. Create a visual signal between the adult and student. An example of a visual signal would be to place your finger aside your nose. When the student observes this, he/she will know that it is time to slow down and think about the action.

437. Ask the student to whisper the directions and quietly read assignments to him/herself. This helps the student focus as they not only see the material but hear it also. This is also helpful when completing assignments with multiple steps. By verbalizing the steps, students often become more conscience of the procedure. Some students are able to stay on task longer if they verbalize the entire assignment while working.

438. Create seating charts. Seat the student near students who are both quiet and independent workers. Provide good role models. Do not seat disruptive students or students that are easily distracted together.

439. Allow the student to keep only the necessary materials for the current assignment on top of the desk. Toys and play objects should remain at home.

Reinforcement and Discipline

Students with special needs and those with ADD are often are more dependent on external reinforcement than other students in the classroom environment. These students also may need more encouragement. Try to reward more than punish. When you see a positive behavior, praise the student immediately. Always avoid ridicule and criticism.

A number of students have difficulty controlling their behaviors. These students may respond to a reward system. If you decide to incorporate a reward system, be sure the student participates in the development of the reward list. For many, an appropriate reward is simply allowing a few extra minutes to socialize with a friend as often these students are the last to finish their work and rarely have extra time.

440. If the student consistently needs to be disciplined during a specific academic area, it is important to check to see if the current adaptations are appropriate. The majority of acting out behaviors tend to occur when the assignment is too difficult.

441. Develop a reward system. Since the student will need continuous and frequent feedback, break the educational day into time blocks. Some students need feedback every five to ten minutes during the initiation of the program. This can easily be done by placing a chart on the student's desk and putting a check or a sticker onto the chart or index card as you walk around the room. Gradually increase time to cover the entire academic block.

442. The class discipline plan is not always an appropriate plan for all students in the class. The student may need a supplemental discipline plan with extra warnings, coupled with a reward system. Whatever discipline plan is used, it is important for the plan to remain consistent for the student throughout the school day. Time Out is often used in response to a behavioral difficulty, or as a proactive measure when problems are about to surface. The Time

Out allows the student time to regroup, have some personal space for a few minutes, or to recover from a temper outburst. It may also allow time for the teacher and the class to regroup and refocus. The goal of the Time Out is to allow the student time to calm down and rethink the situation. Frequently, Steps 1 and 2 can be used as a preventative and proactive strategy for students. Adults often take a Time Out when experiencing a stressful situation. An adult may get a drink or water, cup of coffee or simply walk out into the hall to regroup. Time Outs should be viewed as a legitimate way to cope with a situation before it reaches a crisis level.

If using Time Outs, provide a specific posted sequence. A common sequence of steps may be:

Step 1 – Time out in a designated classroom area.
Some teachers call this area the "Thinking Area". This area, usually located in the classroom, is appropriate for all students who need a few minutes to think something through without interruption.

Step 2 – Time out outside of the classroom area.
Sometimes a student needs to leave the classroom environment. Often teachers work collaboratively to provide a supervised location in a separate classroom.

Step 3 – Time out with a counselor or principal.
This allows the student to cool down and work through the situation with a person who was not directly involved with the situation.

Step 4 – Telephone call home.

443. A token system is appropriate for some students. Tokens may consist of small laminated paper shapes, buttons or beads. You may choose to make your own. With a token system, the student is responsible to keep the tokens in their desk and redeem the tokens for a reward. In the beginning students tend to work for rewards that can be

easily obtained. Encourage the student to set goals and work towards a larger reward.

444. With the student, create a list of reinforcement activities. The student may choose from these activities when their individual goal has been met. What motivates an adult probably will not motivate the student. Create the list together and keep the rewards simple. Some suggestions may include stickers, pencils, pens, basic school supplies, ten extra minutes on the computer, five minutes of free choice activity with a friend, or a coupon for one "excused" homework assignment.

445. An inexpensive way to obtain trinkets for elementary students is to attend garage sales. There are many small items that can be purchased for five cents or less. Another option is to send form letters to large companies asking for donations. Often companies have promotional items they will send to you free of charge.

446. Keep the parents informed when the student has shown improvement during the day. Create a list of positive sayings such as:

Awesome Day!
I discovered the secret to success today!
Super Star!
I'm a Great Student!
Wow!

Photocopy the sayings onto fluorescent paper and laminate them. Cut into strips. Place these strips into an envelope. When the student has a good day, he or she may choose a laminated paper strip to take home. If proper guidelines are set, the older student will be able to monitor his or her own progress. This is also an easy way to communicate with parents daily.

447. Keep parents informed about the reward system used in class. Parents often will provide additional reinforcement in the home.

448. A daily report can be used to monitor behavior and academic goals. An easy way to create a daily report is to tape an index card to the student's desk. Subjects can be added to the card as they are presented during the day. For younger students a happy face may be placed on the card if the student has reached the expected goal during the time block. For older students a rating scale of 1-5 may be used. This report may be sent home daily to increase communication between the school and home.

449. A daily log has proven successful for coordinating home and school communication. Both parents and teachers can use this log to write comments, concerns and suggestions. The student is rewarded by the parent(s). Do not begin a narrative log unless you are sure you will have the time to complete it daily. A daily log is very time consuming, especially when comments usually need to be written at the end of the day or class period when there is usually confusion and chaos.

450. Teach the student to use positive self-talk. "I can do this!" "I can handle this!" or "I'm good at this!" are all examples of self-talk. When you hear a student using negative self-talk or putting him or herself down, stop the student and help the student to rephrase the comments positively.

"Children need love, especially when they don't deserve it!"

Harold Hulbert

"Don't worry if you fall flat on your face....at least you're moving in the right direction!"
Source Unknown

Afterword

People learn in many different ways. Some people learn by reading, whereas, others learn through observation and implementation. Nowhere has it been stated that inclusive education is easy! You will encounter roadblocks when setting up the program and you will discover workable solutions. You will try many new strategies. Some will be easy to implement and others will be complex. Some will prove successful and others will not work as anticipated. I hope, though, with the use of this book, the transition will be smooth and accommodations are easier to make.

You have taken the first step. You have read this book. Now it is time to take the next step. I encourage you to take it. The next step will make a difference in the lives of many children. It is the students' right to be in the classroom and it is our job, as professionals, to provide the most appropriate program possible within the least restrictive environment.

In 2000, this book was revised and updated. Although material has been added and expanded upon, the original numbering of strategies remain the same. This was intentional so those who have previous editions may continue to use their books collaboratively with the new edition.

Keep in mind that inclusive education is a systematic change that does not occur overnight! Change is often gradual. I do believe in several months you will look back, with satisfaction, at the progress that has been made. Good luck! You will make a difference in the lives of many!

Ω

Appendix

Developing An Inclusive Education Program
Checklist

☐ Develop a vision!

☐ List the benefits and possible barriers of an inclusive education program in your school. Worksheet #3.

☐ Visit inclusive education sites

☐ Target a specific grade level in which to develop your program.
_____Grade level
_____Number of students

☐ Fill out the information on the Student Data Sheet. Worksheet #5.

☐ Group the students. Worksheet #7.

☐ Determine the number of paraprofessionals and the total number of paraprofessional hours needed to implement the program. Worksheet #8.

☐ Create an outline of a tentative schedule. Worksheet #10.

☐ Present the plan! Worksheet #11.

☐ Survey the staff for inservice needs. Worksheet #12.

☐ Discuss classroom set up and teaching styles with the volunteer inclusion teachers. Worksheet #13.

☐ Use the follow-up surveys to determine program needs.
Student Survey-Worksheet #14
Parent Survey-Worksheet #15
Paraprofessional Survey-Worksheet #16
Staff Survey-Worksheet #17

Benefits and Barriers
Example

Use Worksheet #3 to write the benefits and possible barriers which may be encountered. The following ideas will help you to get started.

Benefits of Inclusion

* Students receive service in the classroom to the greatest possible extent.
* Students are no longer labeled because they leave the classroom to attend a special class.
* Students can participate in all instructional activities with proper accommodations, even though the outcome may be different.
* Students do not lose valuable academic learning time transitioning between regular education and special education classrooms.
* Students no longer need to work within two fragmented educational systems.
* Students are not pulled in so many directions. Related services are provided within the classroom setting as much as possible.
* The special education teacher develops a better understanding of the classroom curriculum. Strategies that meet the needs for the student in one academic area may be transferred to other academic areas.
* Students become more accepting of one another regardless of the limitations.
* The special education staff can assist other students within the classroom setting if needed.
* Communication increases between regular education and special education.
* General education teachers have more flexibility. They do not have to wait for students to return from their special class in order to begin a new lesson.

Possible Barriers

* Scheduling difficulties.
* Grouping of students.

Inclusion:
Benefits and Possible Barriers

Benefits:

Barriers:

Student Data Sheet Example

	Student's Name	Disability	Paraprofessional Time	Minutes of Service in Accordance with the Student's Individualized Education Plan						
				Reading	Written Language	Math	Social/ Emotional	Speech/ Language	OT/PT DAPE	Other
1	Mary	LD		300	150	300			OT 60	
2	John	MMI	1500	300	300	300		90	DAPE 60	
3	Lynn	LD		150	150					
4	Jake	LD				300		60		
5	Joey	LD		300						
6	Heidi	OHI	600	300	300	300		90	OT 60 PT 60	Health 300
7	Amy	LD		300						
8	Mike	LD		300						
9	Steve	BD	300				300			
10	Frank	VI	300	300	150					Enlargement 60
11	James	LD			300					
12	Alicia	LD				300			OT 60	
13	Mark	BD					300			
14	Tim	LD		300	300	300		90		

Student Data Sheet

			Minutes of Service in Accordance with the Student's Individualized Education Plan						
Student's Name	Disability	Parapro-fessional Time	Reading	Written Language	Math	Social/ Emotional	Speech/ Language	OT/PT DAPE	Other
1									
2									
3									
4									
5									
6									
7									
8									
9									
10									
11									
12									
13									
14									

Student Groupings
Example

Use this form to assist with the grouping of students. Group the students into the least number of classrooms possible. Make several copies of Worksheet #7 and experiment with various different groupings.

GIVEN THE HYPOTHETICAL GROUPS ON WORKSHEET #3, THE STUDENTS WERE GROUPED IN THE FOLLOWING WAY.

Classroom #1   Approximate level _____

❒ Consultation   ❒ Special Education Paraprofessional   ❒ Special Education Teacher
                    (2 hours per day)   (consultation only)

     1. Lynn - LD   2. Brandon - LD   3. Steve - BD   4. Paul - LD   5. Aaron - HI

(One possible reason for this grouping is that the students receive minimal amount of academic service. All of the students should be able to receive their direct instruction from the general education teacher. Steve has a pupil paraprofessional written into his IEP for approximately 1 hour per day. This paraprofessional could help to support the other four students during this time. A paraprofessional would be beneficial for one hour per day to assist the group with reading and written language. This paraprofessional would be scheduled at a different time than the BD pupil paraprofessional to provide extended coverage for all. Brandon receives service for language. If the language service is incorporated into the classroom, the teacher would be able to support the other students with curriculum vocabulary also.)

Classroom #2   Approximate level _____

❒ Consultation   ❒ Special Education Paraprofessional   ❒ Special Education Teacher
                    (2 hours per day)   (1 - 2 hours per day. Includes related
                                                     support services.)

     1. Heidi - OHI   2. Joey - LD   3. Mary - LD   4. Mike - LD   5. Amy - LD

(This group of students receives a greater amount of service than the previous group. Three of the students receive service for reading only. Heidi and Mary have the greatest academic needs. Heidi has a pupil paraprofessional assigned to her for two hours per day. This person will be able to support Heidi along with the students who need reading support. In this classroom the students also receive support for occupational therapy and physical therapy. The occupational therapy could be incorporated into the written language block so assistance may be provided to others if needed. A special education teacher will need to provide direct service for instruction in this classroom.)

Classroom #3   Approximate level _____

☐ Consultation   ☐Special Education Paraprofessional   ☐ Special Education Teacher
                                    (Full time pupil support)   (1-2 hours per day including related
                                                                                                                              support)

1. Frank - VI   2. Mark - BD   3. John - MMI

(In this group, John has a full time paraprofessional assigned to him. Mark was placed in this group so his behavior goals may be monitored throughout the day. Frank will need many modifications due to his visual impairment. This is the only class that has a full time paraprofessional. It would be appropriate to place these three students in the same classroom. Due to the special requirements, the special education teacher will be involved on a daily basis. These students do receive related services. The pupil paraprofessional will need to take breaks and have lunch when a related support person is able to support the classroom.)

Classroom #4   Approximate level: _____

☐ Consultation   ☐Special Education Paraprofessional   ☐ Special Education Teacher
                                                                                                                    (1 hour plus related services)

1. Tim - LD   2. Jake - LD   3. James - LD   4. Alicia - LD

(In this group the service will vary. Several of the students receive OT services, speech and language and will also need support in academic areas. There is no paraprofessional assigned to this group so you would try to incorporate the related services into the curriculum as much as possible.

These groups could be changed in many ways. Since three of the classrooms in this hypothetical situation have pupil support from paraprofessionals, the students could possibly be grouped into three classrooms and the inclusion support could be redistributed, allowing for maximum coverage throughout the day. The students could be grouped by services received or math skills. The grouping and scheduling process will take time. Always keep in mind that no matter how many times you group and regroup the students, you may never find a perfect group, but you will find a group that is manageable.

Student Groupings

Use this form as a worksheet and as a guide with student grouping. Group the students into the fewest number of classrooms possible. You will need several copies of this worksheet. Experiment with various groups.

Classroom #1   Approximate level _____
❏ Consultation   ❏Special Education Paraprofessional   ❏ Special Education Teacher

Classroom #2   Approximate level _____
❏ Consultation   ❏Special Education Paraprofessional   ❏ Special Education Teacher

Student Groupings

Classroom #3   Approximate level _____
❏ Consultation   ❏ Special Education Paraprofessional   ❏ Special Education Teacher

Classroom #4   Approximate level _____
❏ Consultation   ❏ Special Education Paraprofessional   ❏ Special Education Teacher

Learning Styles
(Group students with similar learning styles into classrooms)

Math and Problem Solving Skills

Low   **Average**   **High**

Related Services

Speech/Language   Occupational   Adaptive Physical   Other Related
Services   Therapy   Education   Services

Classroom #1   Classroom #2   Classroom #3   Classroom #4

Paraprofessional Minutes

(Calculate the amount of paraprofessional time as carefully as possible with the information you currently have. Build 15 minutes of daily consultation time into the schedule.)

Classroom #1
Pupil Inclusion Paraprofessional
(assigned to a specific student)
Student contact time: _____
Consultation time: _____
Lunch: _____
Break: _____

Inclusion Program Paraprofessional
(assigned to a classroom of students)
Student contact time: _____
Consultation time: _____
Lunch: _____
Break: _____

Total Minutes: _____

Classroom #2
Pupil Inclusion Paraprofessional
(assigned to a specific student)
Student contact time: _____
Consultation time: _____
Lunch: _____
Break: _____

Inclusion Program Paraprofessional
(assigned to a classroom of students)
Student contact time: _____
Consultation time: _____
Lunch: _____
Break: _____

Total Minutes: _____

Paraprofessional Minutes

Classroom #3
Pupil Inclusion Paraprofessional
(assigned to a specific student)
Student contact time: _____
Consultation time: _____
Lunch: _____
Break: _____

Inclusion Program Paraprofessional
(assigned to a classroom of students)
Student contact time: _____
Consultation time: _____
Lunch: _____
Break: _____

Total Minutes: _____

Classroom #4
Pupil Inclusion Paraprofessional
(assigned to a specific student)
Student contact time: _____
Consultation time: _____
Lunch: _____
Break: _____

Inclusion Program Paraprofessional
(assigned to a classroom of students)
Student contact time: _____
Consultation time: _____
Lunch: _____
Break: _____

Total Minutes: _____

Sample Schedule for an Inclusive Setting

This schedule is currently used in an inclusive setting. Students are cross-categorically grouped by reading abilities. The seventeen students receive service from one full time special education teacher with three additional hours of paraprofessional support. Four language arts groups (approximately 90 minutes) take place in the morning. Please note how time blocks are staggered for instruction time and also for specials (music, technology, media, physical education), allowing the special education teacher to better serve the setting.

Daily Schedule

8:00 - 9:00	IEP Meetings, preparation, communication and planning time.
9:00 - 9:30	Communication with general education teachers. (Changes in daily lesson plans. Overview of schedule. Sign up for flexible time).

Morning Block

Classroom #1 4 Students	Classroom #2 4 Students	Classroom #3 5 students	Classroom #4 4 Students
9:40 - 11:15 Lang arts block **Spec. Education Tchr.** Supplemental curriculum provided by the special education department when classroom assignments are inappropriate or cannot be modified.	**9:40 - 11:15** Social Studies and Science block. Movies, large group instruction, story, break. Activities that do not require the assistance of the special education department.	**9:40-11:15** Reading and language arts block with the **Paraprofessional** Reteaching, adaptations to the curriculum and support. Direct instruction is provided by the general education teacher.	**9:40 - 10:40** Specials: Music, gym, art, technology, and media. - - - - - - - - - - - - - - - **10:40-11:15** Large group instruction, spelling, break. Activity that does not require the assistance of the special education department.
11:15 - 12:00 Specials: Music, gym, art, technology, and media. - - - - - - - - - - - - - - - **12:00 - 12:30** Handwriting, spelling practice, get ready for lunch. No special education support is provided during this block.	**11:15-12:20** Reading and language arts block with the **Spec. Education Tchr.** Supplemental curriculum provided by the special education department when classroom assignments are not appropriate.	**11:15 - 12:20** Movies, large group instruction, story, and break. Activities that do not require the assistance of the special education department.	**11:15-12:30** Reading and language arts block with the **Paraprofessional** Reteaching, modification to the curriculum and support. Direct instruction provided by the general education teacher.

Sample Schedule for an Inclusive Setting

12:30 - 1:00

Lunch for the general education teachers, special education teacher and paraprofessional
The paraprofessional moves to another program for the afternoon.

In the afternoon, the special education teacher is available from 1:00 –2:15 to support students. General education teachers sign up for the time in advance for additional support during the two staggered time blocks. At 2:35 students are grouped for a team taught math class. An additional fifteen minutes are allocated at the end of the day to check on individual students.

Afternoon Block

1:00 - 2:15 Social Studies/Science large group activities. - - - - - - - - - - - - - - **1:00 - 1:45** **Special education teacher is available** on a sign up basis. This should be done 1-2 days in advance.	**1:00 - 1:45** Specials: Music, gym, art, technology, and media. - - - - - - - - - - - - - - **1:45 - 2:15** **Special education teacher is available** on a sign up basis.	**1:00 - 1:45** Specials: Music, gym, art, technology, and media. - - - - - - - - - - - - - - **1:45 - 2:15** **Special education teacher available** on a sign up basis.	**1:00 - 2:15** Social Studies/Science large group activities. - - - - - - - - - - - - - - **1:00 - 1:45** **Special education teacher available** on a sign up basis.
1:00 - 2:15 This time block is "flexible time" for the special education teacher. The general education teachers will let you know in advance when you will be needed. A sign up sheet should be provided to the general education teachers.	This daily time block allows you to provide support across the curriculum for the students. Read the IEP to be sure students are receiving the allocated amount of service. If not, some of this time may be needed-to meet the IEP requirements.	**Suggestions** for this time block may include: - Alternate forms of testing for spelling, math, social studies and science. - Team teaching or support for social studies and science activities may be incorporated.	- Drill and practice activities that support the curriculum. - Planning time and consultation with general education teachers that have preparation time during this time block. - A paraprofessional available during this time would be a definite asset.

2:35 - 3:35 Math
In this schedule, the students are grouped for math. All students that have and Individualized Education Plans are grouped into one classroom. In this sample schedule there are 7 students who received math services. The math block is team-taught daily.

3:35 - 3:50
Check outs and homework assignments are monitored during this time.

Preliminary Schedule Worksheet

Daily Schedule

Notes:_____

_____

_____

Morning Block

Classroom #1 __ Students	Classroom #2 __ Students	Classroom #3 __ Students	Classroom #4 __ Students
_____ Time	_____ Time	_____ Time	_____ Time
Time	Time	Time	Time
Time	Time	Time	Time
Time	Time	Time	Time

Preliminary Schedule Worksheet

Daily Schedule

Notes: _____

_____

_____

Afternoon Block

Classroom #1 __ Students	Classroom #2 __ Students	Classroom #3 __ Students	Classroom #4 __ Students
_____ Time	_____ Time	_____ Time	_____ Time
_____ Time	_____ Time	_____ Time	_____ Time
_____ Time	_____ Time	_____ Time	_____ Time
_____ Time	_____ Time	_____ Time	_____ Time

Presenting the Plan

Place the following materials into an information packet:

* A brief summary of the proposal.

* Advantages and possible barriers to inclusive education. Worksheet #3.

* List of the target group of students and the grade level information.

* Student data sheet. Worksheet #5.

* An approximate calculation of the number of paraprofessionals and the hours you will need. Worksheet #8.

* Tentative schedule outlines. Worksheet #10.

* Other data you have collected that will support the program.

Staff Survey
Inservice Needs

The following survey will assist the Special Education Department in determining the needs of the building staff in relation to inclusion.

	Disagree				Agree

1. I understand the concept of inclusive education.   1 2 3 4 5

2. I am willing to participate in an inclusive education program.   1 2 3 4 5

3. I would like to have a group of students with disabilities in my classroom.   1 2 3 4 5

4. I will need additional training and inservice before accepting a group of students.   1 2 3 4 5

5. I would like to receive training in the following area: (Please check all that apply.)

    More about Inclusive Education   ❑
    Collaboration Skills   ❑
    Curriculum Accommodations   ❑
    Working Effectively with Paraprofessionals   ❑
    Disability Awareness Information   ❑
    Other: (Please write below).   ❑

_____
_____
_____
_____

Please write any comments or suggestions and return this survey to me. Thank you very much.

Classroom Setup Checklist

(Use the following questions as guidelines.)

Planning. What time of day would be best to meet informally? When planning larger units or lessons, when would be a good time to meet? Who will take responsibility for planning?

Lesson format. How will the lessons be taught? Who will take responsibility for daily planning? What type of teaching system will work for all involved? How will the lessons be presented and by whom?

Responsibility. Who will be responsible for the students' grades? What grading system will be used? How will the modifications affect the grade? Who will be responsible to make the modifications and to hold the student accountable for classroom assignments?

Classroom routines. What are the classroom routines? Pencil sharpening? Bathroom breaks? Turning in assignments?

Classroom discipline. Who will be responsible for classroom discipline? What is the discipline plan? Will all students use the same discipline plan? What are the rewards and consequences?

Additional comments or concerns that should be addressed:

Student Survey

1. **How do you feel about your class placement?**

2. **How do you feel you are performing in the classroom?**

3. **Are you following the classroom rules?**

4. **Are the academic modifications to the curriculum helping you?**

5. **Are you receiving enough support in the classroom?**

6. **Are you able to complete the classwork and the homework assignments?**

7. **How do you get along with the other students in your classroom?**

8. **Are you involved in extracurricular activities? If the answer is no, which extracurricular activities would you be interested in?**

_____
Signature/Date

Parent Survey

1. What are your reactions and feelings to your child's new placement?

2. How does your child feel about the new placement?

3. How is your child coping with the academic demands of the classroom?

4. How would you rate your child's self esteem in this setting?

5. How do you feel your child interacts with his/her peers?

6. What changes have you noticed (positive or negative) in your child since the new placement?

7. Can you suggest any ideas or strategies that may assist us when working with your child?

Additional Comments:

_____

Signature/Date

Paraprofessional Survey

1. How do you feel the students are performing in the classroom?

2. Do you have any specific concerns about the students?

Student's Name   *Area of Concern*

3. Do you feel you receive sufficient guidance from the Special Services department? If not, please list suggestions for improvement.

4. Do you feel you have adequate time to communicate with both general and special education teachers?

5. Do you have suggestions for specific modifications or adaptations?

6. What types of training would you like to receive?

Additional comments, questions, or concerns that should be addressed:

_____

Signature / Date

Staff Survey

1. How are the students performing in your classroom?
   Academically- (If a student is experiencing difficulty, indicate the student and
      specific area.)

   Social/ Emotional-(How are the students interacting with their peers?)

**2. Are the students completing daily classwork and homework
   assignments?**

3. How are the students' work habits and study skills?

**4. How do the students respond to the current behavior management
   system?**

5. How do you feel the placement has affected the students' self esteem?

6. How is the communication system working for you?

7. In general, are you satisfied with the students' progress in your class? Are you comfortable with the number of students in your classroom?

8. What solutions would you have to any of the problem areas mentioned above?

9. What changes would you like to see in the program?

Additional Comments:

_____

Signature/date

Curriculum Accommodations
Student Worksheet

Student's Name:_____ Grade _____ Date _____

Team Members:_____

Step 1: List the student's strengths
_____
_____
_____

Step 2: List the goals
_____
_____
_____

Step 3: Ideas and Strategies for Accommodations

Textbook:
_____
_____
_____

Daily Assignments:
_____
_____
_____

Written Language:
_____
_____
_____

Spelling:
_____
_____
_____

Mathematics:

_____
_____
_____

Organizational Skills:

_____
_____
_____

Directions:

_____
_____
_____

Large Group Instruction:

_____
_____
_____

Classroom Assessments:

_____
_____
_____

Classroom Behavior:

_____
_____
_____

Other areas of concern:

_____
_____
_____

*Person responsible for the modifications:

Textbook:_____	**Daily Assignments:**_____
Written Language:_____	**Spelling:**_____
Mathematics:_____	**Organizational Skills:**_____
Directions:_____	**Group Instruction:** _____
Assessments:_____	**Behavior:**_____
Other:_____	

*Special education teacher, general education teacher, inclusion paraprofessional, peers, volunteers, related service personnel (OT, PT, DAPE), other school personnel - e.g. art, physical education, technology, music, or media specialists.

Overview of
Curriculum Accommodations

Student's name:_____ Date:_____

Homeroom teacher:_____

Special Education teacher:_____

Note the accommodations that will need to be made for the student in the following areas. Fill in the name of the person responsible to create the modifications. Make copies of the completed form and distribute the copies to all team members. If no accommodations are needed at the present time, leave the area blank. Accommodations may be added at a later date.

Textbook / Person Responsible:

_____
_____
_____
_____

Daily Assignments / Person Responsible:

_____
_____
_____
_____

Written Language / Person Responsible:

_____
_____
_____

Spelling / Person Responsible

_____
_____
_____
_____

Math / Person Responsible:

_____
_____
_____
_____

Directions (Oral and Written) / Person Responsible:

_____
_____
_____
_____

Testing Procedures / Person Responsible:

_____
_____
_____
_____

Large & Small Group Instructions / Person Responsible:

_____
_____
_____
_____

Organizational Skills / Person Responsible:

_____
_____
_____
_____

Textbook Accommodations
Student Worksheet

Student's name: _____ Date of Planning Meeting: _____

Subject:_____ Grade:_____

Team Members
Name: Title:

_____   _____

_____   _____

_____   _____

_____   _____

Please check all that apply to the individual student.

☐ **The student will need the accommodations to the classroom textbook.**
    ☐ The student should read all classroom texts with a peer or with a small group.
    ☐ Audiocassettes should be provided to the student.
    ☐ The entire textbook should be provided on audiocassettes.
    ☐ The entire textbook should be paraphrased for the student.
    ☐ Alternating pages of the text should be recorded for the student.
    ☐ _____
*Person responsible for accommodation:_____

☐ **The student will need the following services.**
    ☐ Preteaching or previewing of the material.
    ☐ Outline of the required text.
    ☐ List of vocabulary words and definitions. A modified list if appropriate.
    ☐ Checklist of required assignments with due dates.
    ☐ Study guide for required assignments.
    ☐ A complete set of textbooks should be provided for home use.
    ☐ _____
*Person responsible for accommodations:_____

☐ **The student will require direct support from the Special Education Department.**
    ☐A supplemental textbook will be needed
        Who will provide the service? _____
        Number of minutes daily? _____
        Time of day service will be needed._____

Accommodations for Daily Assignments
Student Worksheet

Student's name: _____ Date of Planning Meeting: _____

Subject:_____ Grade:_____

Team Members

Name: | Title:

_____ | _____
_____ | _____
_____ | _____
_____ | _____

Please check all that apply to the individual student.

☐ **The student will need assistance with daily assignments.**
    The student will be able to complete daily class assignments with the following accommodations:
    ☐ Modify the length and grading of the assignment.
    ☐ Allow the student to work in cooperative groups.
    ☐ Allow the student to complete the assignment orally.
    ☐ Allow a peer to read and write the student's ideas.
    ☐ Allow the student extra time to complete the assignment.
    ☐ _____
    ☐ _____

*Person responsible for accommodations:_____

_____

☐ **The student will need the following supplemental services.**
    ☐ A checklist of assignments and due dates.
    ☐ A complete set of textbooks for home use.
    ☐ A photocopy or a consumable book.
    ☐ _____
    ☐ _____

* Person responsible for accommodations:_____

_____

❑ **The student will require direct support from the Special Education Department.**

    ❑ Assignments provided at a lower readability level.

    ❑ Supplemental curriculum or adapted materials will be provided covering the same skill area.

        Amount of service daily? _____

        Approximate time of service?_____

* Person responsible to provide the service:_____

❑ **The student is unable to complete the assignments assigned to the class.**

    ❑Supplemental assignments will be provided in accordance to the student's Individualized Education Plan.

    ❑ The student has a Special Education Paraprofessional written into the Individualized Education Plan.

        Amount of service daily? _____

        Areas of special concern._____

        _____

    ❑ Ideas for supplemental materials.

    _____

    _____

    _____

* Person responsible to provide the service:_____

Additional comments:

Accommodation Log Sheet

Date	Strategy #	Results

Daily Observation Worksheet

Student's Name	Observed Behavior	Comments

ASSIGNMENT LOG

NAME:_____   WEEK OF:_____

SUBJECT	MONDAY	TUESDAY	WEDNESDAY	THURSDAY	FRIDAY
READING					
ENGLISH					
MATH					
SOCIAL STUDIES					
SCIENCE					
REMINDERS					

BEHAVIOR CONTRACT

STUDENT:_____   DATE: _____

TEACHER: _____SUBJECT / CLASS PERIOD:_____

I will demonstrate the following behavior(s) in the classroom:

_____

_____

_____

_____

_____

I would like to work toward the following:

Goal:

_____

_____

_____

Incentive:

_____

_____

_____

Additional Comments:

_____

_____

_____

_____   _____
Student Signature / Date   Teacher Signature / Date

Copies:
      Student   Parent
      Teacher   File

Glossary

abstract thinking - ability to think in terms of ideas.

accommodation – changing the topic, product, activities or feedback checklist without lowering or changing the standard.

adaptation - the process of changing the performance package to meet the curricular, resource, or student learning needs.

ADA - The Americans with Disabilities Act 1990. This legislation requires employers and businesses working with the public to accommodate individuals with disabilities. Schools receiving public funds must make reasonable accommodations using it's own financial resources and discrimination cannot take place, regardless of the disability.

ADD - see Attention Deficit Disorder

alternative assessment - an evaluation using various methods in place of traditional paper/pencil tests to assess a student's knowledge. Demonstrations, oral presentations or projects are some examples.

Attention Deficit Disorder - a condition in which a student has difficulties in directing or maintaining attention to normal tasks of learning.

auditory blending - blending of sounds into words.

auditory discrimination - ability to hear differences and similarities in spoken word.

auditory memory - ability to recall information that is heard.

authentic assessment – evaluating a students' performance with meaningful tasks related directly to the curriculum taught.

behavior - a relationship between a stimulus and a response.

behavior modification - the process which creates a change in the stimulus/response pattern.

collaboration - to work together towards a common goal.

configuration cues - the outline of a word in relation to the shape and length.

contract - a written agreement between teacher and student that outlines specific behaviors and consequences.

demonstration – assessment in which the student actively shows what they have learned in a manner other than a paper/pencil test.

discrimination - ability to differentiate between visual, auditory, tactual, or other sensory stimuli.

distractibility - attention that is easily removed away from the task.

expressive language - vocal, gestures and/or written expression.

fine motor - use of small muscle groups for specific tasks such as handwriting.

hyperactivity - excessive activity in relation to others of the same age and in similar situations.

IDEA - the Individuals with Disabilities Education Act (formally P.L. 94-142 - The Education for the Handicapped Act).

IEP - See Individualized Education Plan.

Individual Education Plan - an individual program designed for a student who qualifies for special education services.

impulsivity - acting or speaking out without considering the consequences.

inclusion paraprofessional - a person who works with a group of students in the inclusive classroom.

inclusion pupil paraprofessional - a person who is assigned to support a specific student. The paraprofessional is written into the IEP.

inclusive schooling - a school setting in which students receive their educational instruction within the classroom setting for the entire or a substantial portion of their school day.

least restrictive environment (LRE)- a term requiring that, to the greatest possible extent, students with disabilities are educated with their non-disabled peers.

memory - recall of visual, auditory, and or tactile stimuli.

mnemonics - visual or word related aids that facilitate retrieval of information.

modifications – lowering or changing the standard to better meet the instructional needs of a student with an IEP or 504 Plan.

parallel activity - an assignment in which the outcome is similar but the materials used to reach the outcome may be entirely different.

portfolio – a collection of students' work which demonstrates what the student has learned over a long period of time.

previewing - reading, listening to, or viewing the selection before instruction or a test.

readiness - physical, mental and emotional preparedness for a learning activity.

remediation - improvement of basic skills.

short attention span - inability to pay attention to something for a long period of time compared to others of the same age.

supplemental teaching - provisions provided to the student in the form of reteaching, reinforcement and/or alternate curriculum when needed.

supportive teaching - modifications made to the classroom curriculum or the environment by the special education teacher or inclusion paraprofessional which will allow the student to experience success in the mainstream.

sound symbol - relationship between the printed form of a letter and the sound.

team teaching - two teachers working together jointly to develop, plan and teach a lesson.

tracking - the practice of grouping students according to their perceived ability.

visual discrimination - ability to perceive likeness and difference in pictures, words and symbols.

Organizations to Assist You!

ARC of the United States
1010 Wayne Avenue #650, Silver Spring, MD 20910
Information 1-301 265-3842 ARCs Publication Desk 1-888-368-8009

The ARC works to improve the lives of all children and adults with mental retardation and their families. They have an extensive publications catalog, which includes fact sheets about specific topics related to mental retardation. Some publications are available in Spanish as well as English. Call for information.

Consortium on Inclusive School Practices-Child and Family Studies Program
Allegheny-Singer Research Institute 320 East North Avenue Pittsburgh, PA 15212

The Consortium on Inclusive Schooling Practices publishes a "Catalog of products from Funded Projects" which includes a list of manuals, articles, videotapes, brochures, and fact sheets produced by investigators who have received grants from the US Dept. of Education, Office of Special Education and Rehabilitative Services. The web site address is: www.asri.edu/CFSP/brochure/abtcons.htm

Institute on Community Integration
102 Pattee Hall, 150 Pillsbury Drive SE, Minneapolis, MN 55455
(612) 624-4512 publications (612) 624-6300 general information

This University Affiliated Program promotes interdisciplinary training, service, technical assistance, research and dissemination activities designed to enhance community services and social support for students with disabilities. Materials are reasonably priced and cover a wide range of topics. Information on inclusion, as well as other topics, is available through newsletters, resource guides, training manuals, research reports, curricula, and brochures. Send for a free catalogue. This is an excellent source for information.

Learning Disabilities Association of America
4156 Library Road Pittsburgh, PA 15234
1-888-300-6710

Learning Disabilities Association of America is a nonprofit national organization that provides public awareness, research, and information about learning disabilities. LDA distributes many booklets and books for parents, children and teachers. Call to request a catalog.

National Center on Educational Restructuring and Inclusion
The Graduate School and University Center   The City University of New York
33 West 42 Street, New York, NY   10036
(212) 817-2090

NCERI promotes and supports inclusive educational programs. NCERI addresses issues of national and local policy, conducts research, provides training and technical assistance. This organization also disseminates information about programs, practices, evaluation and funding of inclusive education programs. Periodic free publications are mailed to those on their mailing list. Call and ask to be added to the list. You will find the information beneficial.

National Information Center for Children and Youth with Disabilities
PO Box 1492, Washington, DC   20013-1492
1-800-695-0285 (Voice/TTD)   1-202-884-8200

NICHCY is a federally funded information clearinghouse that provides information on disabilities and disability-related issues. This organization also provides clearly written booklets and resource listings regarding special education services. This excellent organization not only provides information to assist educators, but for parents, professionals and caregivers as well. Feel free to call this organization with any questions you may have in relation to children and youth with disabilities.

National Library Service for the Blind and Physically Handicapped
Library of Congress 1291 Taylor Street NW Washington, DC   20542
1-800-424-8567

The National Library Service distributes reading materials in alternate formats (Braille, audiotape) to US citizens who are blind or have a physical impairment that prevents them from using ordinary printed materials.

Special Education Resource Center (SERC)
25 Industrial Park Road   Middletown, CT   06457
(860) 632-1485

SERC provides annotated bibliographies and resource listings regarding inclusion. It is a resource for professionals, families and community members regarding early intervention, special education and pupil services, and transition-to-adult life for individuals with special needs. If you are interested in receiving the bibliographies or resource listings, call the librarian at SERC. This organization is happy to assist you.

The Association for Persons with Severe Handicaps (TASH)
29 West Susquehanna Avenue, Suite #210, Baltimore, MD   21204
(410) 828-8274   FAX (410)-828-6706

This international organization advocates for persons with disabilities to be fully included in the school, work, and community environment. TASH holds annual conferences, publishes both a monthly newsletter and quarterly journal. If you would like to receive some free samples of the publications or would like membership information, feel free to call or fax your request to the above number.

Telephone and Web Site Addresses

Disclaimer: The following telephone numbers and web site addresses are current at the time of press. Although listed as resources, Peytral Publications, Inc., does not endorse nor guarantee the accuracy of the information at these sites.

Organization & Phone numbers	*Web site address (when available)*
ACCESS Eric 1-800-538-3742	www.accesseric.org
ADA Information Center 1-800-949-4232	www.adainfo.org
American Association on Mental Retardation 1-800-424-3688	www.aamr.org
American Council of the Blind 1-800-424-8666	www.acb.org
American Speech-Language-Hearing Association 1-888-321-ASHA	www.asha.org
American Society for Deaf Children 1-800-942-2732	www.deafchildren.org
Arc of the United States 1-301-565-3842	www.thearc.org
Associated Services for the Blind Resource 1-215-627-0600	www.libertynet.org/asbinfo
Auditory-Verbal International Inc 1-703-739-1049	www.auditory-verbal.org/
Autism Society of America 1-800-328-8476	www.autism-society.org
Children and Adults with ADD (CH.A.D.D.) 1-800-233-4050	www.chadd.org
Closing the Gap	www.closingthegap.com
Educational Resources Information Center Clearinghouse on Disabilities Gifted Education 1-800-328-0272	http://ericec.org
Kids on the Block 1-800-368-5437	www.kotb.com
Learning Disabilities of America (LDA) 1-888-300-6710	www.ldanatl.org
Multiple Sclerosis Society	http://www.nmss.org
National Association for Parents of Children with Visual Impairments 1-800-562-6265	www.spedex.com/napvi

National Alliance for the Mentally Ill 1-800-950-6264	www.nami.org
National Clearinghouse on Postsecondary Ed for Individuals with Disabilities 1-202-939-9320	www.acenet.edu/about/programs
National Down Syndrome Society 1-800-221-4602	www.ndss.org
National Information Center for Children and Youth with Disabilities (NICHCY) 1-800-695-0285	www.nichcy.org
Office of Special Education Programs (OSEP)	www.ed.gov/offices/OSERS/IDEA/index.html
National Information Center on Deafness 1-202-651-5051	www.gallaudet.edu~nicd
National Federation of the Blind (NFB)	http://www.nfb.org
PACER Center (for families of children & adults with disabilities) 1-800-537-2237	www.pacer.org
Recordings for the Blind and Dyslexic 1-800-221-4792	www.rfbd.org
Spina Bifida Associations of America 1-800-621-3141	www.sbaa.org
Teacher's Edition Online	http://teachnet.com
United Cerebral Palsy Associations, Inc 1-800-872-5827	www.ucpa.org

If you need additional help in locating an organization, contact NICHCY (National Information Center for Children and Youth with Disabilities) at 1-800-695-0285. For a more extensive list of toll free numbers, order the NICHCY publication entitled National Toll-Free Numbers.

Resources for Special Education

The following pages include several reference books and videos for educators, parents and students.

The following three publications are companion books to **Inclusion: 450 Strategies for Success.**

Inclusion: A Practical Guide for Parents – Moore

This component helps parents understand the inclusive setting and provides the necessary tools to promote and enhance their child's learning. The book includes specific exercises to assist with reading, math, writing and attention skills. Many strategies, exercises, questionnaires, checklists and do-it-yourself graphs assist parents in helping their child benefit from learning experiences both at school and in the home.

Inclusion: An Essential Guide for the Paraprofessional – Hammeken

This practical publication includes comprehensive information written specifically for the paraprofessional. There are hundreds of strategies and reproducible material to help paraprofessionals daily working in inclusive settings. This book can be used for staff development. Reproducible forms.

Inclusion: Strategies for Working with Young Children – Moore

A companion to *Inclusion: 450 Strategies for Success,* this book contains a gold mine of information. This book of developmentally based ideas and written to help children between the ages 3 and 7. Communication, large and small motor development, pre-reading, writing, and math, plus activities to help children learn about feelings, empathy resolving conflicts and problem solving. This is an excellent resource for educators in early childhood settings to second grade. Reproducible forms.

The full-page cartoons in the book **Inclusion: 450 Strategies for Success** are available for staff development and training. Each of the following books contains more than 100 cartoons. These cartoons may be reproduced as transparencies for staff development!

Ants in His Pants – Absurdities and Realities of Special Education. 1998 Michael F. Giangreco

Flying By the Seat of Your Pants – More Absurdities and Realities of Special Education 1999 – Giangreco

Teaching Old Logs New Tricks – Absurdities and Realities of Education -Giangreco

Collaborative Practices for Educators – Lee

This practical book will help educators improve personal and group communication skills. The 180 practice activities can be used individually, with a colleague or in a group setting. The Appendix includes a reproducible set of the popular *Tip Cards for Effective Communication.*

Complete Guide to Special Education Transition Services – Peirangelo

An outstanding reference that covers: procedures; rights; current laws; school responsibilities; organizations; forms; legal requirements; parent responsibilities; state and government agencies and more. Organized into 13 sections with 12 appendices.

Early Intervention Dictionary – A Multidisciplinary Guide to Terminology

This excellent publication defines hundreds of medical, therapeutic and educational terms commonly used in the early intervention field. This invaluable dictionary helps parents and early intervention professionals successfully understand one another and collaborate more effectively.

Inclusion: The Next Step – Wendy Dover Staff Development Training Video Series

> **Tape 1 Building Consensus for Inclusive Education.** Tape 1 will help you to understand the scope of inclusive education today; build consensus among staff members; address barrier issues; and utilize effective strategies for managing resistance.

> **Tape 2 Understanding Your Inclusion Options** Tape 2 helps you to navigate the options for accommodations; evaluate accommodation ideas and strategies for students; realize the significance of six primary accommodation levels; and work modifications into the general curriculum.

> **Tape 3 Planning Effective Modifications and Accommodations** Tape 3 will help you to structure student accommodations and curricular modifications; tackle the tasks of instructional planning and program planning; communicate effectively; put planned accommodations into action.

> **Tape 4 Delivering Necessary Support** Tape 4 will help you to promote collaboration among teachers and support staff; allocate crucial instructional and curricular materials; put consultative and pull-out resources to work in your program; maximize the effective use of paraprofessionals.

Inclusive High Schools-Learning from Contemporary Classrooms – Fisher, Sax & Pumplan
This book provides a framework for developing inclusive high schools by taking a detailed account of high schools, their struggles and ultimately their success. Topics discussed include: building school based relationships, developing support strategies, preparing the classroom, planning lessons, adapting curricula and more. Appropriate for high school teachers, administrators and university professors.

How to Reach & Teach All Students in the Inclusive Classroom – Rief & Hamburge
This valuable resource for educators (grades 3-8) is filled with ready-to-use strategies, lessons, and activities that will help meet the academic, social and emotional needs of the diverse populations in the general education setting! Learn how to reach students through their multiple intelligence, develop portfolios, manage behaviors, and more. Over 100 full page reproducible management tools.

Lessons and Activities for the Inclusive Primary Classroom – Kennedy
Written to help K-3 general and special educators successfully integrate children with special needs into the classroom. The 122 lessons with reproducible activities cover social skills, communication, arts, math, science, social studies, physical education and more. Individual performance objectives and projects can be used individually or with the entire class.

Let's Write - Stowe
Includes over 200 activities and 110 worksheets to help students (grades 3+) who are having writing difficulty. Beginning with simple words and progressing to increasingly complex writing, this book takes into account all ability levels and learning styles. Grades 3+

Phonemic Awareness: Lessons, Activities and Games – An Educator's Guide - Scott
Help struggling readers! Research indicates that many students with reading deficits lack phonemic awareness skills. Research also indicates that these skills can be taught! Use this publication to develop sound relationships as a prerequisite to reading or to supplement the current reading curriculum. Includes and overview of phonemic awareness principals, 48 scripted lessons – ready for immediate use, 49 reproducible masters and progress charts. Grades K-4.

Phonemic Awareness: The Sounds of Reading – Staff Development Training Video
This companion video to the book *Phonemic Awareness: Lessons, Activities and Games* demonstrates the basic components (identification, comparison, segmentation, blending and rhyming) of phonemic awareness and shows how to apply these techniques not only to reading, but to all subjects. Excellent staff development video! 25 minutes

Special Kids Problem Solver – Shore
This excellent publication provides information and strategies to recognize and respond effectively to 30 common problems encountered including; math anxiety; reading disabilities; aggression; ADD; AIDS; HIV and more. All levels

The Special-Needs Reading List – An Annotated Guide to the Best Publications for Parents and Professionals
In one easy-to-use volume this publication reviews and recommends the best books, journals, newsletters, organizations and other information sources on children with disabilities. An invaluable resource for schools and libraries.

Teaching Kids with Learning Difficulties in the Regular Classroom – Winebrenner
This is a perennial best seller with ideas and strategies for all age levels. The book contains a wealth of information and includes many reproducible masters! A must have for every school.

Teaching Reading to Children with Down Syndrome: A Guide for Parents and Teachers – Oelwien
This nationally known reading program ensures success by presenting lessons that are both imaginative and functional. The lessons can be tailored to meet the needs of each student. Although written for students with Down Syndrome, this publication will help others struggling readers as well. 100 pages of reproducible material!

Teenagers with ADD – A Parent's Guide
This best seller helps both teachers and parents understand and cope with teenagers with ADD. The book extensively covers symptoms, diagnosis, treatments, accommodations, family and school life, advocacy and more.

Tough to Reach, Tough to Teach – Students with Behavior Problems – Rockwell
Prepare for encounters with disruptive, defiant, hostile students by knowing how to defuse undesirable behaviors and structure "face saving" alternatives. This book offers lists of tips covering the following areas: setting limits, arranging the classroom for safety, and maximizing personal effectiveness. A valuable resource for general and special education teachers

CORWIN PRESS

The Corwin Press logo—a raven striding across an open book—represents the union of courage and learning. Corwin Press is committed to improving education for all learners by publishing books and other professional development resources for those serving the field of PreK–12 education. By providing practical, hands-on materials, Corwin Press continues to carry out the promise of its motto: **"Helping Educators Do Their Work Better."**